By Phil and Steve Mahre
with John Fry

NO HILL TOO FAST

SIMON AND SCHUSTER

NEW YORK

Copyright © 1985 by Phil Mahre, Steve Mahre and John Fry
All rights reserved
including the right of reproduction
in whole or in part in any form
Published by Simon and Schuster
A Division of Simon & Schuster, Inc.
Simon & Schuster Building
Rockefeller Center
1230 Avenue of the Americas
New York, New York 10020
SIMON AND SCHUSTER and colophon are registered trademarks of
Simon & Schuster, Inc.
Designed by Stanley S. Drate/Folio Graphics Co., Inc.
Manufactured in the United States of America
10 9 8 7 6 5 4 3 2 1
Library of Congress Cataloging in Publication Data
Mahre, Phil.
  No hill too fast.
  1. Ski racing. I. Mahre, Steve. II. Fry, John,
DATE. III. Title.
GV854.9.R3M34   1985   796.93   85-14235
ISBN: 0-671-55706-8

This book is dedicated to our wives,
Holly and Debbie, for their understanding
and patience throughout our careers.

ACKNOWLEDGMENTS

We would like to recognize the key people who helped us not only with this book but throughout our careers.

The two most important people are our parents, Dave and Mary, whom we thank for their guidance and support. They were never pushy, but always there when help and direction were needed in our lives.

We want to thank all those who helped in our early competitive years of learning. They are too numerous to mention here, as are all the coaches, teammates, and equipment suppliers who gave us encouragement and help over the years.

A special word of thanks is due to Hank Tauber, who kept everything in order during our early years with the U.S. Ski Team; to Harald Schoenhaar for his emotional support, friendship, and terrific coaching; to Ed Chase and Alan Trimble, devoted friends and equipment reps; and to Dr. Dick Steadman for his hard hours of miracle work on our legs.

For this book we are indebted to the many photographers whose pictures appear here and who followed our careers, but especially to Tom Lippert for the time he spent looking through his lens to take the scores of photos used in the instruction sections of the book.

Finally, our thanks to John Fry for the patience and hard work it took to put this all on these pages.

Phil and Steve Mahre

CONTENTS

INTRODUCTION   11

ONE
SARAJEVO: 1984   17

TWO
TWO IS BETTER THAN ONE   77

THREE
HOW TO GROW YOUNG SKI CHAMPIONS   127

FOUR
THE U.S. SKI TEAM   173

FIVE
LEARNING HOW TO WIN   197

SIX
MODERN MEDICINE AT WORK   247

SEVEN
STRUGGLE FOR THE WORLD CUP   295

EIGHT
ALL THE WAY TO THE BANK   337

NINE
THE BEST IN THE WORLD   365

How to Ski the Mahre Way

1 LEARNING TO SKI: A NEW APPROACH   43

2 PHASES OF THE TURN   93

3 THE TECHNIQUES OF TURNING   145

4 PREPARING YOUR SKIS TO SKI, AND CANTING   223

5 THE TACTICS OF SKIING   263

6 INTEGRATING TECHNIQUE AND TACTICS   317

7 SKIING ICE AND BUMPS, AND OTHER TIPS   351

INTRODUCTION

The international world of ski racing is not an especially promising arena for American athletes. Most of the big races—like Kitzbühel's Hahnenkamm and the annual Arlberg Kandahar—are held in Europe. That is where the American skier must spend the winter in order to compete against the world's best. With the exception of two weeks when the World Cup tour comes to the United States, we lack the home-field advantage. Instead, we have to live in a multilingual, itinerant world where a racer awakes in the morning and has to figure, "If this is Monday, it must be St. Anton."

Until 1981 no American had ever won the World Cup, the most difficult of all the Alpine ski trophies to win because it means a racer must succeed in not just one race but a couple of dozen competitions held over four months in at least ten countries. Beyond that, no American man had ever won an Olympic gold medal in skiing.

If American men were ever to succeed in ski racing, coaches and officials believed, we would first have to create a massive base of competitors. Then the best athletes would surface to the top, imitating successful U.S. programs in swimming and tennis.

In the early 1970s, therefore, it would have been laughable to predict that America's first Alpine World Cup would be won by a twenty-four-year-old with a profound indifference to programmed training, growing up with a twin brother who would be the second-best skier in the United States. It was an outrageous contradiction of two widely heralded principles of how the United States should succeed: that the national ski team must be built on a wide pyramidal base of athletes across the land, and that winning is the result of motivating individuals to perform in carefully structured training programs.

As we grew up at the bottom of a ski lift of a little-known resort called White Pass in Washington's Cascade Mountains, we found our own way to win races. Unfortunately, ours is a story that corporate Olympic executives and institutionally trained coaches continue to ignore.

Our record of winning in a sport where consistent first-place results eluded American male competitors for forty years is a story from which readers can draw many conclusions about how success is achieved. In some ways we are a reminder of the message implanted in Herrigel's *Zen in the Art of Archery:* if you think forever of winning, victory will elude you. For us, winning an Olympic medal was not the most important thing in life. And yet, for having this opinion, we were criticized at the 1984 Winter Games by a press and public whose only interest was the capture of gold medals.

Our success as skiers stems from a technique that is elegantly simple. Its basis has only started to become clear to teachers in the last few years. Ignored by millions of skiers, this technique, like most applied skills, originates with an understanding of the tool the skier brings to the sport—a flexing beam with curved sides called a ski. We believe that if you apply the edge of this tool correctly to the snow, you will understand how to improve your skiing ability. We ask only that you focus on the skills of skiing: balance, weight transfer, edge pressure, and think less of your progress through the conventional stages of skiing such as getting from a snowplow to parallel. By way of sequential illustrations and carefully thought-out pointers and exercises, we will make you a better skier.

Many of the ski training drills shown in this book are actually used by the U.S. Ski Team in preparing for the World Cup. They were developed largely by our coach, Harald Schoenhaar, and we have adapted them for use in recreational skier clinics, the Mahre Training Centers started at Keystone, Colorado, in the winter of 1984–85.

In a lifetime spent on skis one or the other of us broke a knee or an ankle or was swept away by an avalanche. We traveled a half-million miles on the international race circuit. We skied the classic resorts of the Alps, went to Japan, and north to the Arctic Circle to the home of our chief competitor over the years, Sweden's Ingemar Stenmark. Through it all we never lost our enthusiasm for one thing—going fast. And if we weren't winning races through love of speed, then we were reveling in it on motorcycles or on water skis.

Speed is contagious. We hope, through reading this book, you become infected. And then you'll start to understand what it's like to ski like the Mahres.

Phil and Steve Mahre
with John Fry

Winter, 1985

A Note by the Mahres' Collaborator

In the past twenty years of reporting and writing about ski racing, I interviewed many of the best athletes on the international scene. The interview I enjoyed most was with Phil Mahre in 1982, just as he was completing the best winter of his World Cup career. It took place at Montgenèvre, a French ski resort on the Italian border near Sestřiere. We talked for four hours—until I ran out of recording tape.

The day before, I had seen him surpass three-time World Cup winner Ingemar Stenmark in the slalom. It was an extraordinary performance. Now, in an empty dining room of the hotel where he was staying, Phil analyzed the mental side of winning.

As he talked, I recalled past interviews with racers who had made the point: the best racers in the world are equal in technique when they stand in the starting gate, but it is the intelligent and determined who win. Now I knew it.

If that interview inspired me to help them write this book, my decision was clinched by the fact that in that same winter, Phil's brother, Steve, placed third in the World Cup standings. I wanted to know the reason for their success.

In a world often seething with estrangement and personal rivalries, it is inspiring to come across two people who grew up in such harmony. The reason, I had assumed, was because they were twins. A recent study, for example, has shown exceptional telepathic rapport between twins. But the study was of identical twins, and the Mahres—though almost identical in appearance—are fraternals. The mystery of such harmony remains.

What I can attest to is that in the dozens of hours of conversation and interviews with Phil and Steve in preparing this book, I failed to uncover an important issue on which they didn't agree. Yet one twin does not parrot the other. If Phil, for example, begins to talk about a particular topic—such as what a youngster must do to make the U.S. Olympic Ski Team—then Steve will chime in with thoughts amplifying his brother's view.

Their mother, Mary, who raised nine children, says that "they grew up inseparable, but they were more like good friends than brothers. The most unusual thing I recall about the twins is that they never bickered. They never made us cry except for happiness."

I once asked Phil if he wanted his son to become a ski racer. He shrugged his shoulders and confessed that, if pressed, he would move to a ski resort so the boy could have the same advantage *he* had as a child. "Of course," Phil confessed, "he wouldn't have the other advantage I had . . . Steve." It was said quietly, as if I already knew what it meant to have such a brother.

The lesson of the Mahres' lives is inspirational: how it is possible for two people to compete fiercely, yet nurture each other. It would be tempting to recite the obvious—"if only the whole world"—but I will refrain. Perhaps, though, the reader of these pages will glean some such magic from the Mahres' story.

John Fry

NO
HILL
TOO
FAST

ONE

SARAJEVO: 1984

It's been said that the hardest decision an athlete has to face is when to quit. Early in the 1983–84 season, with no misgivings, we decided to retire from ski racing. Serge Lang, the florid, giant-sized journalist who is the dynamo behind the World Cup, urged us not to leave, but only a million-dollar guarantee would have kept us going another season, and that wasn't about to happen. A future career in the sports business was.

The winter of 1984 was the fiftieth year since American skiers started to compete internationally in Alpine racing. For ten of those years—one fifth of the era of modern competition—we raced as members of the U.S. Ski Team. But for all our successes racing on the World Cup circuit—unprecedented for Americans—we were facing the fact that no male skier from the United States or Canada had ever won a gold medal in Olympic downhill, slalom, or giant slalom. The 1984 Olympics would be at Sarajevo, Yugoslavia, in February.

The covers of *Sports Illustrated* and the national ski magazines showed us carrying America's medal-winning hopes, despite the fact that the 1983–84 racing season was turning out to be the poorest in our careers. We were skiing like has-beens, continuing to race on the circuit mainly in the hope of finding our form again

At Sarajevo, the Olympic flame was lit. It was our last chance for a gold medal.
TOM LIPPERT

before the Olympics, and because our contracts with ski equipment manufacturers stipulated that we must race to earn our base salaries.

Pride was a factor too. Three World Cup championship seasons, a gold medal at the World Championships in 1982, and a silver at Lake Placid had set up a platform of achievement from which we were finding it hard to step down. But for every athlete there has to be an end to winning. We had read all the stories about Muhammad Ali and Terry Bradshaw and Reggie Jackson, athletes who kept on competing after their prime. It was hard to accept that this was happening to us.

The harsh reality of it became evident in the press conferences at Sarajevo. We knew exactly what we were capable of doing, but we also acknowledged the challenge, considering the fact that in a dozen pre-Olympic World Cup races one or the other of us had placed in the first ten only twice. So we told the truth—we said that we weren't necessarily expecting to win a gold medal. But what the press heard us say was that we weren't really *trying* to win a gold medal.

In skiing it's hard to figure what's wrong when you aren't winning. Slalom and giant slalom are two-run events. You have to race down two separate courses, each with fifty to sixty gates marked by pairs of flagged poles in the snow. Each gate demands a precise turn—precise, that is, because one of the secrets to winning a ski race is to travel the shortest distance from the starting gate to the finish line. But it isn't the only secret. Often the shortest distance traveled by the racer is not necessarily the fastest. You have to figure and feel the fastest line down the course; you have to learn the places where you can carry speed in a transition from steep to flat. It's a mental juggling act carried on at speeds up to fifty miles an hour over an abrupt span of a minute to a minute and a half.

After you finish your run down the first course, assuming you manage not to fall or straddle a pole, you must have a fresh strategy for your run down the second course. That strategy depends largely on how far you wind up ahead or behind the other racers in the first run. If you're leading you may ski conservatively in the second run

After ten years on the international race circuit, and three World Cups, Phil had determined to retire after the 1984 season.

RUSSELL/K2

and give up a few fractions of a second to a couple of other racers. In the end the guy who wins the gold medal is the one whose combined time for the two runs is fastest.

In the vocabulary of Alpine ski racing, slalom and giant slalom are called "the technical events." For good reason. You not only have to ski well, you have to ski with as few errors as possible. To do this your head has to be flushed clean, be free of distractions. Call it concentration. In 1984 we lacked it. Our thoughts were too much on what would happen to us after we retired. And back in Arizona, Phil's wife, Holly, was expecting a baby. Phil recalls: "Normally, my personal life doesn't affect my skiing. But I was glad I didn't know what was happening at home until after the slalom at Sarajevo was over. It would have been nearly impossible to focus on what I had to do."

The slalom traditionally is the last race of the Winter Olympics. Before it took place at Sarajevo, on Sunday, the U.S. gold medal drought had ended. First, Debbie Armstrong—a Pacific Northwest skier like ourselves—had won the women's giant slalom, the first woman gold medal winner from the United States since Barbara Ann Cochran in 1972. Then Bill Johnson became our first male gold medalist in Alpine, winning the downhill. Prior to the race, Billy had used his big mouth to put pressure on himself. After he won a training run on the Sarajevo downhill, he announced himself a sure winner. Johnson said the other racers might as well pack up their skis and go home.

Like Bill Johnson, we put pressure on ourselves, but with us it's an inward psyching: "I'm better than anyone today. No one can beat me on this kind of hill." Bill, on the other hand, lets it be known on the outside, and it upsets a lot of people. Yet by announcing what he's going to do, he generates the psychic pressure he needs to produce. (Actually, he never had talked that way until he won his first downhill at Wengen in January, before the Olympics.)

Bill's predicting that he would win the downhill affected the way people saw us. In press conferences Johnson exuded confidence and a will to win. We appeared negative about our chances.

Johnson had reason to talk the way he did. In repeated training runs he had been fastest down a course virtually identical to the

Bill Johnson predicted he would win the downhill. He had reason to talk the way he did. So did we.

PETER MILLER

one he would race for the Olympic medal. But slalom is totally different from downhill. You don't know what the course will be like until the day of the race when the gates are set, and even then there is no such thing as a trial run down the course.

Nevertheless, Johnson did what no American had done before, and he deserves a lot of credit. He had announced his intention to win a gold medal, and he went out and did it.

Meanwhile, we knew our chances of doing well in the giant slalom, the most difficult of the Alpine disciplines, were not good simply because we hadn't done well in it that season. In giant slalom you can be as aggressive as you want, but if you're not on the right line and skiing correctly, you're going to finish low in the standings. In slalom you can do a lot wrong, but aggressiveness can still win.

Our giant slalom skiing was weak in 1984, medal chances slim. Nonetheless, Phil's eighth place at Sarajevo was his best result of the winter.   TOM LIPPERT

As it was, we placed eighth and seventeenth in the giant slalom at Sarajevo, the best we'd done together all season.

It's hard to explain why a ski racer wins or loses. Phil says, "When you're winning, it always seems effortless. You get to the bottom and find yourself in first place. But the season of 1984 was sure different. When I got to the bottom in any run, as often as not I was in tenth place, or worse."

Our old coach, Harald Schoenhaar, who later would be named head Alpine director of the U.S. Ski Team in the fall of 1984, was at Sarajevo. He had coached us almost from the day we joined the ski team back in 1974 and he knew our skiing inside out. "You're skiing technically well," he said, "but there's just no punch to it."

You feel like you're skiing the same as you always have—you try and you try—and nothing happens.

We studied videotapes over and over, attempting to figure out what was wrong. We looked better on tape than we felt when we were skiing. In the giant slalom it appeared we were making nice carved turns, our body actions looked smooth, yet no one could see what was wrong. Only we could feel it. Unfortunately, the tapes couldn't show whether we were pressuring the edge of the ski at the critical split second when it was needed.

Skiing is not like golf or tennis. If something's wrong, a Jack Nicklaus or John McEnroe can compare his swing today with what he was doing when he was winning. In ski racing the technique and equipment change too much from year to year. You can look at a videotape of yourself in the winning season of 1981 three years later and it won't be especially relevant if your skis are different and the slalom gates have been changed from solid poles to ones that hinge at the snow level, or any number of other different circumstances.

This was the situation going into the slalom at Sarajevo. We wanted to win as much as anyone, but millions of Americans watching on television at home already had us pegged as losers. Billy Johnson looked like a winner, and so did the girls' team. U.S. Ski Team Alpine Director Bill Marolt, currently athletics director at the University of Colorado, was giving informal press conferences stressing the importance of "a winning attitude." We, on the other hand, were saying that it's wrong to push a winning attitude down to the level of youngsters who haven't experienced the consistency that goes with winning. So in addition to being seen as scorning the value of a gold medal, we were perceived as being at odds with the leadership of our own ski team.

A gold medal is valued differently inside the Athletes' Village at the Olympics—not the way the press and television see it. You can find the spirit of the Olympics, the honor of competing, in the rooms and places where athletes from different countries meet, not in the glare of television lights. Nothing would have been easier at Sarajevo than for us to say at the press conferences that the most important thing in our lives was to win a gold medal. The public

U.S. Ski Team Alpine Director Bill Marolt wanted a winning attitude, but we believed that more was involved.

SKI MAGAZINE

would have loved it. But it would have been dishonest. Still, we secretly harbored the hope of an Olympic win before our racing careers ended.

While we hadn't been optimistic at all about winning the giant slalom at Sarajevo, the slalom was different. First of all, the Olympic slalom has a record of upsets. An unknown Spaniard, Fernando Ochoa, won it at Sapporo in 1972. Pepi Stiegler of Austria, now the ski school director at Jackson Hole, Wyoming, had not been expected to win in 1964, least of all to be followed closely by Billy Kidd and Jimmy Heuga, the silver and bronze medal winners.

The other reason for hope was that Steve had come close to winning a couple of slalom races before the Olympics:

"In January, I actually—or nearly—won a World Cup slalom in Europe.

"One of the disadvantages of being nearly identical twins, however, is that we frequently get mistaken for one another.

"It happened in a race at Parpan, in Switzerland, just a couple of weeks before Sarajevo. A ski team coach, Tom Kelly, was partly to blame, along with myself, for not checking the start list. Before the race started, by error, Kelly gave me Phil's numbered bib. I recorded the fastest time, but we were disqualified on the technicality of wearing the wrong start numbers.

"The next day I felt confident again. Incredibly, though, in the very next race after the bib screw-up, my binding pulled out of a ski. It had happened to me maybe once before in ten years of racing on the World Cup circuit. Still, I didn't let this odd series of events get me down. In fact, I felt really good about my slalom. I felt that any day I was going to pop one open."

Phil, meanwhile, was less positive but saw a glimmer of hope. "Throughout the season I hadn't felt really centered on my skis. Sometimes I was too much on the tips, sometimes on the tails. But I had a couple of races where everything could have gone right. In Bulgaria, just before the Olympics, I uncorked a very good first run in slalom. I knew that if I could put two good runs together, I could win. That's the essence of racing the technical events—putting two good runs back-to-back."

And there was a third factor that lifted our chances of doing well in the slalom at Sarajevo. Of six World Cup slalom races held before the Olympics, five had been won by Ingemar Stenmark and Marc Girardelli. Neither racer was eligible to compete at the Olympics.

Stenmark was ineligible because after the Lake Placid Olympics he had elected to take out what is called an FIS B License, created by the Federation Internationale de Ski, governing body of ski racing. The B License enabled Ingemar, a Swede and our nemesis for ten years on the World Cup circuit, to cut his own endorsement deals with companies. He was not required—as were we—to have income from product endorsements come through his national ski federation. He hired his own business agent. Then, like Bjorn Borg, he established a residence in Monte Carlo for tax purposes. He could still race on the World Cup circuit and in the FIS World Championships, but, effectively, three years before, he had signed away his right to compete in the 1984 Winter Games by taking out the license.

The FIS abolished the B License before the Olympics, opening up the possibility that Stenmark might be allowed to ski at Sarajevo. But the International Olympic Committee would have nothing to do with it.

It's hard to understand how the FIS could create the B License and three years later rescind it as if it never had existed. If the other racers were smart, they'd take the FIS to court. In the four years after Lake Placid, Stenmark has made millions, while everyone else has had to stick by the rules and work through their ski federations.

Girardelli's case was slightly different, but the effect was the same. Marc is a young Austrian dominated by his father, Helmut. He's a brilliant slalom racer, but sometimes it's hard to know how he's achieved so much. In one race we remember, Marc was among the first five finishers in the first run. In the second run he ran into trouble. About fifteen gates from the finish he spun out of the course, his run ended. He said in his broken English, "I better talk to my *vater* before he comes talk with me."

Three-time World Cup winner Ingemar Stenmark contracted himself out of the Winter Games, though there were last-minute efforts to get him reinstated. JOHN FRY

Meanwhile, we had placed second and fourth. Helmut Girardelli came and congratulated us. Then he walked right by his own son as if he didn't see him. Marc was in tears. We couldn't believe it.

Earlier he had difficulties with the Austrian ski training program. His father pulled him out of the program and arranged for him to race for Luxembourg. Since he was still an Austrian by citizenship, however, he couldn't race in the Olympics. As a result, we were in a race in which two of the favorites had dropped out.

The morning of the slalom the clouds lifted on Mount Bjelasnica, but you would never have known it down in the valley in Sarajevo. We still couldn't see the mountains because of the smog.

Also out of the Games was Marc
Girardelli, a brilliant slalom racer and the
successor to ourselves and Stenmark
at the head of the pack.

Girardelli's father was a tough tutor.
When his son lost one race, Helmut
walked coldly by him and congratulated us.

It was a long bus ride up switchback roads to the race site. We recalled the initial problems of the buses at Lake Placid in 1980 as we rode up from the Athletes' Village. After the opening ceremonies we had had to hitch a ride in a van to get back into town. Eventually, transportation was straightened out. But at Sarajevo, though the buses ran, it often took an hour and a half to get up to the mountain. And when the race was over, the spectators had to walk a half mile back down the mountain to find a bus to take them home.

Above the smog of the town the hill shone brightly. We had liked it from the time we first saw it. In fact, it had some of the quality of the slalom hill at Whiteface Mountain at Lake Placid—steep and constant in pitch. It had a final *steilhang,* or steep face, which had caused grief to a number of top racers in the giant slalom five days earlier.

Riding up the lift, then skiing down to where the slalom would start, we noticed the hill was still icy from the water sprayed on it for the giant slalom. But as we sideslipped alongside the slalom course, it seemed the snow on the slalom hill itself wasn't that hard. It was hard-packed old snow—grippy, like man-made snow.

The other feature we noticed about the slalom was that it was a long hill for the number of gates set: sixty in the first run and fifty-eight in the second. Looked at another way, the vertical drop was the absolute maximum under the FIS rules: 200 meters, or more than a 600-foot drop in elevation from the top to the bottom of the hill.

The number of gates was not unusual, but set on a smaller hill they would have resulted in what we call a "tight" course. Here, because of the distance, the gates were relatively far apart for a slalom. The result was what we call a "turny" course. So we could see there'd be no advantage, as there is in some slaloms, going straight at the poles. On most of the gates we would be making complete turns, clearing the inside pole of the turn with the body.

This much we figured out. Would the others?

You'd never think so after watching their first runs. No less than seven of the fifteen best slalom racers in the world fell and didn't finish or were disqualified. Most of them made the mistake that we had avoided: they went straight at the poles. Right away, they got into trouble. They either skied out of the course or wound up jamming their edges when they saw they weren't going to make the turn in the next gate.

Some of their troubles stemmed from the "rapid gate," introduced a couple of seasons ago. Unlike the old, rigid slalom poles, the rapid gate hinges at the snow level. It is less punishing to the racer when he hits it, and it results in fewer delays in holding ski races because the poles don't come out of the snow.

Many racers have come to believe that you don't have to ski around the new rapid-gate poles, you can go directly at them. Those who believed that at Sarajevo, on a steep hill, found themselves sadly wrong. In our view you have to go around the pole. If you don't—if you go straight—you end up having to jam your edges and make a turn across the hill that slows you to a stop. Or you slide. Or you lean in, instead of making a turn that keeps your speed going. That's what happened at Sarajevo.

The rapid gates created other problems. Several racers, including Jonas Nilsson, the Swede—who was second fastest in the first run and could have won the bronze medal—and Tiger Shaw of the U.S., experienced trouble with their goggles. The reason was the same. Tempted to go straight at the rapid gates, the racers actually crossed the poles with their bodies. The pole scraped across their faces and often dislodged their goggles. When the racer couldn't see where he was going, he had to use his hands to push the goggles back into place and lost time.

Some racers have attempted to overcome this problem by using a gummy substance to prevent the goggles from sliding around. The real solution, however, is to target your feet to go outside the pole. The racers who ignored this lesson at the Olympics lost. In the first run they included the Italian slalom star Paola de Chiesa; Michel Canac of France; Max Julen, who had won the gold medal in the giant slalom; Franz Gruber, the best slalom racer on the Austrian team; Andreas Wenzel, the 1980 World Cup winner; and Paul Frommelt, a potential gold medal winner.

Steve's first run in the slalom at Sarajevo was dazzling. He had a half-second lead and virtually a sure shot at the gold medal.   TOM LIPPERT

Steve raced third and looked by far the best of anyone in the field. "I really skied the bottom steep face well. As for Phil, he had to start eleventh in the ruts. It was quite something for him to be third fastest in the first run, seven tenths of a second behind me."

The sun was shining and things were looking good. Even before the race the support from friends helped. Harald Schoenhaar told us we were skiing slalom very well and that we could win.

Dick Steadman, the world-famous orthopedic doctor who performed the difficult knee and ankle surgery that literally kept us ski racing until 1984, was there. Two years earlier he had operated on Steve. After the surgery he said, "Those are gold medal knees, go and win on them." Steadman had that much confidence in us. Having him at Sarajevo meant a lot.

Thom Weisel, the president of the U.S. Ski Team, was there. Thom is our financial adviser and a good friend. Phil remembered that he'd won at every World Cup meet that Thom ever attended. It was a good omen.

Then, back in Phoenix, Arizona, at 1:35 A.M., an hour before the race got under way in Sarajevo, Phil's wife, Holly, gave birth to an eight-pound son. We didn't know it. Holly believed it was a sign that something special would happen in Sarajevo.

Going into the second run, we knew we were good for gold and silver if we just stood up. Though Jonas Nilsson had recorded the second-fastest time in the first run, we suspected that nerves were going to get to him. A relative rookie at twenty-one, Nilsson would have difficulty handling a situation in which the whole world would be watching him, whereas we had competed in this kind of scene before.

Phil was convinced about winning the silver medal. "I didn't think anyone would outski us in the second run. My main thought was to hit the first six gates well and set the tempo for the rest of the race. I did.

"On the final steep pitch I really stomped on my skis. When I pulled into the finish I knew I had the silver medal. I also knew I probably wouldn't beat Steve unless he made a major mistake."

Going into the second run, Steve possessed what in slalom is considered an almost insurmountable lead: seven tenths of a second. With Nilsson's second run error, it was hard to see how he could lose.

With Steve poised to start at the top, Phil radioed up from the finish area what he'd learned about the new course set for the second run. The last thing Phil had on his mind at that moment was the television cameras, but of course they were beaming the picture back to that huge American TV audience this last day of Olympic competition and evidently it blew a lot of people's minds— the idea of one brother advising the other how to beat him. For us it was routine: each was always trying to help the other do his best, even if it meant being beaten in the process. Which one of us won

First one down the course radioed to the top. At Sarajevo the instructions were, "Catch the first six gates—and carry the tempo into the rest of the course."

TOM LIPPERT

wasn't the important thing—let's just say that neither of us could have been as good as he was without the other's support.

Phil recalls what he radioed up the hill: "Catch the first six gates with round turns and carry the tempo into the rest of the course. Remember the gate on the knoll where a late turn might cause you to get low? It isn't as bad as it looks. On the bottom face it's slick, so get on and off your edges quickly."

It was good advice, but Steve had another problem on his mind. "I had such a big lead going into the second run that I really could approach it one of two ways. I could ski carefully, cleanly, let six or seven guys beat me, and still have a chance to win the overall race.

Or I could go all out. I said to myself, 'No, you can't take a chance. You have to win both runs to be the true champion.'

"My mistake was in wanting to win too badly. By the fifth gate I got behind, and by the sixth I was sliding. I lost time, but it wasn't drastic. I recovered some speed on the next half-dozen gates. I thought to myself, 'You lost maybe 15/100ths of a second back there, but the race is still yours to win.'

"Then I got to the flush—a series of gates set vertically down the fall line of the hill and not open to the racer's line of attack. I entered it too straight. I was racing fifth, so there was already a rut in the flush. My inside ski tip, instead of climbing out of the rut, fell off. Suddenly I had more weight on the inside ski than I wanted. I was

Steve's second run at this gate looked good, but it turned out to be a nightmare. TOM LIPPERT

locked in, and had to throw the ski around in a wild turn. I probably lost a half second.

"It was a nightmare.

"From then on I knew I had to ski all out to have a shot still at the gold medal. But on the last pitch, where Phil had done well, my hand got back. I rotated too far and just about stopped.

" 'You dumb ass,' I said to myself at the finish. I realized then that there had been no need for me to ski the way I had. I could have contented myself with a clean, solid run. Instead, I had gone all out to win."

Our dad, Dave Mahre, said that half the gold medal belonged to Steve. Phil agrees, but for other reasons.

"Dad said, 'That's half your brother's medal.' It really is. Not only in the sense of his bad run, which gave me the win, but also in the sense of our whole careers. Even without Steven's mistakes, I couldn't have put the gold medal around my neck alone. He was always there helping me over the years.

"As I watched him come down the course I could see that every mistake he made increased my chances of winning. But you never wish for anyone to fall in a race, least of all your brother."

In the end, 57 of 104 racers fell in the Olympic slalom. Was it a hollow victory? You're asking the wrong guys if you want an answer to that one. Let's just say that we rose to the occasion, and the others didn't.

The excitement around the finish line was hysterical. The press, who'd written thousands of words predicting we wouldn't win, hounded us for statements. Microphones were shoved in our faces. Finally we left to go to the doping control station. Here the first four finishers, plus other racers selected at random, had to supply urine samples showing no trace of drug usage for the competition. From doping we went to the ski room where our technical rep, Ed Chase from K2 Skis, would wax and pack our skis for transportation back to the States. Then we found a van to get us to the Athletes' Village as fast as possible.

We were in a rush to get to the medal ceremony in Sarajevo. We stripped out of the colorful pants and sweaters of the team uniform

Press and television reporters besieged Phil at the finish line. "That's half your brother's medal," our dad said.
TOM LIPPERT

and took showers. Clothed again, we went downstairs to find a bus into town. At the exit door Donna de Varona and a television crew from ABC were waiting for us.

"Phil, your wife has had a baby!" she cried.

"I was stunned. Here I was on camera and the birth of my child was being announced. She told me that my wife, Holly, had had a boy a few hours earlier. It was crazy. She gave me a phone number to call in Phoenix. I said, 'Thanks.' As I walked off I started crying. It was too much."

We drove in a van into Sarajevo. A huge crowd had gathered in the public square in front of the terrace where the medals would be presented. We were hustled into a back room. There, on a giant TV monitor, we could see Gunde Svan and the cross-country skiers, just outside, receiving their medals. We would follow.

Before we went out they asked if we wanted to put makeup on for the cameras. We said, "Forget it." Then we walked onto the outdoor stage, with the crowd below. Marc Hodler, the president of the FIS, was there, and Chick Igaya, the Japanese skier who won a silver medal in slalom in 1956. They presented our medals.

The loudspeaker played "The Star-Spangled Banner," and the Stars and Stripes were raised on two poles. The French Tricolor went up on the third pole, representing the bronze medal won by France's Didier Bouvet.

Steve found it the most emotional trophy presentation he'd ever attended. "I had to bite my lip to hold back the tears. I was standing

The medal presentation ceremony was the most emotional we've ever attended—and different. The U.S. was on the victory stand.

LORI ADAMSKI-PEEK

behind Phil, who was on the higher stand facing the flag, and I was thinking I might be in his place. 'That could have been you up there,' I said to myself. But I wasn't as mad as I had been just after the race."

Phil recalls, "It was different, because I had always raced for myself and not anybody else before. Now all of the U.S. was up there on the victory stand. I had won the World Cup three times, but that achievement was recognized almost exclusively by people in the sport of skiing. The gold medal would be different."

After the medal ceremony we retreated inside, away from the noise of the huge crowd cheering in the square. The medals hung from ribbons around our necks. We were taken to a couple of press conferences. Phil found it brutal.

"One reporter asked me which was more important, a gold medal or a baby? I said it was a ridiculous question. They asked me what role my wife played in my career. Here I was celebrating a gold medal and they were pushing personal questions completely off the subject at hand. I became quite emotional—in fact, I cried. My feelings were confused. So when I was asked a perfectly sensible question about the slalom itself, I was in tears and couldn't answer."

We left the press conferences and headed to the ice stadium for the closing ceremonies of the fourteenth Winter Olympiad. The delegation of American athletes had elected figure-skating champion Scott Hamilton to carry the flag of the United States into the stadium. Scotty said, "This is Phil Mahre's day. He won a gold medal and had a baby boy, so he should carry the flag."

That typifies not only what kind of a guy Scotty is, but what the Olympic spirit is all about.

"It was a big, big moment for me to carry the flag. After the ceremony it was pandemonium. We ate at the Athletes' Village. Steve hit the sack, but there was no way I could sleep. We were invited to a party by ABC. I went with Pete Carruthers and Scotty Hamilton. We talked to Roone Arledge about getting ABC to cover a skating event Scotty would host in his hometown of Bowling Green, Ohio. We also talked about having a reunion of the Olympic athletes at Lake Powell in 1986. The party went on into the early hours. I was so wired up about the gold medal and my baby boy, I couldn't sleep.

"Having my son born on the day of winning a gold medal was like a storybook tale. My wife, Holly, is a twin, like me. She is from Scottsdale. We met at a ski-shop appearance I made in Phoenix in 1980. We were signing autographs. I saw Holly standing across the aisle of the shop. It was weird, because the first thing I said to myself was, 'I'm going to marry that girl.'

A couple of hours before the race, Phil's wife, Holly, gave birth to a son. Afterward, he learned about it in a television interview.

TOM LIPPERT

"Her family invited us to dinner that night. Afterwards, we kept in touch by mail, and she joined me on the World Cup tour in 1981. We were married in 1982, and in December our daughter, Lindsey, was born. Then on February 19, 1984, that last day of the Mahres' last Winter Olympics, our son, Alexander, arrived.

"I got back to the Athletes' Village as dawn was breaking. We breakfasted, packed our bags, and left for the airport. From Sarajevo we flew to Zurich, where we spent the night. The next day I flew on to Phoenix, where I saw my two-day-old son for the first time. We returned as a family to the World Cup circuit in Aspen and Vail, Colorado, where I would race for the last time in my career. Finally we came home to Yakima, Washington.

"I look at my baby boy and wonder if he will be a ski racer like me. Probably not. Very few have enjoyed the kind of upbringing we had. The chances of my son doing what I've done are slim.

"Steven and I literally grew up at the bottom of a ski hill, forty miles west of Yakima at White Pass. As a twin I had another advantage that few, if any, ski racers can ever have. It was the constant competition and coaching from Steven that made my victories possible. And at Sarajevo, in an odd way, he had done more than his usual share to make my gold medal possible."

HOW TO SKI
THE MAHRE WAY

Section 1 begins a series of illustrated articles on the Mahre ski
technique, which appear alternately with chapters
of their life story.

LEARNING TO SKI: A NEW APPROACH

Skiing down a mountainside requires body movements essentially no different from walking or running. That's easy to say and sounds obvious, but the fact is that natural foot-to-foot movements in skiing are lacking in at least nine out of ten people we observe on ski hills today. What is wrong?

There are several explanations. First, after mastering the basic skills of getting from the top to the bottom of a hill on short skis at modest speeds, most people abandon ski instruction. The scenery and the exhilaration of moving downhill understandably become satisfactions in themselves, and many skiers don't persist with their lessons. Lack of instruction produces lack of technique. Even longtime skiers suffer if they don't return to ski school occasionally because they may still be using out-of-date techniques never designed for present-day equipment.

A second reason for the prevalence of so much bad skiing today is that popular ski technique still embraces a holdover from the past. The notion persists that the beautiful—or correct—way to ski is with the skis parallel and the two feet moving together in perfect synchronization. Top competitors have not skied this way for a number of years, but most recreational skiers either don't relate to the way racers ski or they see photographs of racers with their skis seemingly turning together without realizing that only one ski is being pressured.

Hundreds of photos—many of them sequenced with a motorized camera— were taken in the preparation of the instruction for this book. Seen on location at Keystone, Colorado, are Steve Mahre with photographer Tom Lippert and the writer John Fry.

Finally a revolution has taken place in the last dozen years in the way skis themselves are made. At one time the design and materials used in skis required the skier to pressure the front of the ski to make it turn. The result was that skiers had to adopt fairly unnatural body positions to turn. The modern ski is different. It allows the skier to stand on the ski in a natural, comfortable body stance, using one leg at a time to bring out the properties in the ski, fore and aft, that cause it to turn.

Believe it or not, the basic techniques we used to win our medals and World Cup races are ones that you can use in your own skiing. In this sense skiing should be no different from any other sport— tennis, for example, where the arm and foot movements of the champions are no different than those of the pupil. There is no valid reason why you shouldn't ski like Phil or Steve Mahre, either. In fact, by skiing our way you will realize a quantum leap in your technique. What we do is not complicated, and the only difference between ourselves and you will be the speed at which we come down the hill.

Even before we retired from ski racing, we were fired by the idea that the training exercises we practiced on the U.S. Ski Team could be applied to teach recreational skiers. In this line of thought we were heavily influenced by our coach, Harald Schoenhaar. We are indebted to Harald for many of the exercises that appear in this book and for his suggestions, which run throughout *No Hill Too Fast.*

While traveling around the world—in Europe, Japan, and throughout North America—we have witnessed, countless times, in thousands of skiers, the same basic shortcoming: failure to pressurize the ski that makes the turn. Time and again we see people skidding turns with both feet. The cause of this almost universal disease in skiing, we have come to believe, is ignorance. It is ignorance of the forces at work in skiing and of the fact that skiing is no different from other land sports that are practiced with quickness and agility and require you to move with independent leg action.

Snow skiing is not like water skiing. Much as we like to water-ski, the sport itself is almost the reverse of snow skiing. Water skiing tends to emphasize locking the feet together and inclining the whole body into the turn to offset centrifugal forces. Skiing, on the other hand, should emphasize independent leg action and the angling of the upper body in opposition to the legs in order to offset the centrifugal forces of turning.

Most of the exercises shown in this book are aimed at getting you, first of all, to find your most comfortable position on your skis and then helping you to work the skis independently of one another. If the approach sounds different or unfamiliar, don't conclude that it is thereby difficult. Quite the opposite. We are asking you only to employ the same natural body movements you use in running when you transfer body weight from one foot to the other. Nature is on your side. And so is the equipment you use to ski with today. The boot, with its laterally stiff sides, and the ski, with its curved side profile and flexing action, have been designed to allow you to ski in this way. If you fail to do so you are not employing the properties that designers have put at your disposal.

We're All Alike

Look at Steve Mahre [*opposite page*] snowplowing and Phil [*above*] making a parallel turn. We're light-years apart in the technique being demonstrated, right? Wrong.

Both of us are applying the single most important fundamental of ski technique: shifting weight onto the ski to pressure its edge.

In the exercise shown here we are shifting weight from one ski to the other. To do the exercise, face downhill and place the skis in a snowplow, or wedge, position. Automatically the skis tilt on their inside edges.

Bending your ankles inward will increase edging and stop you from moving downhill. Flattening the skis by flexing the ankles outward will let the skis slide forward down the hill.

Maintaining the snowplow position, flatten the skis and let them slide forward. Now shift weight onto one ski by tipping the upper body over it. The added pressure on the ski will make it "want" to turn.

Quickly shift weight to the other ski. Continue plowing downhill, shifting weight from one ski to the other.

Beginners are not the only ones who should use the snowplow. From time to time it can help an advanced skier to recapture subtle feelings for pressuring and edging the skis. It also is a helpful exercise when you are trying out new skis and boots. By moving slowly and shifting weight from ski to ski, you can begin to gain a feel of how your body should adapt to the turning properties of the new equipment.

Now look at Phil skiing parallel. Basically the only difference is that his skis are not in a wedge configuration. His body weight has been placed on the outside, turning ski, which throws up some snow because of the force generated by his speed.

Like the snowplower, the parallel skier should apply pressure on one ski at a time. Weight transfer is complete.

As in running, shifting weight from foot to foot is the basis of modern skiing.

Weight Shift Creates the Turn

Whether we're making the classic snowplow turn or turning in the gates, the principle of independent leg action remains the same.

In the snowplow turn [*opposite page*] the upper body leans out to transfer weight onto the turning ski. The combination of downhill motion, pressure on the edge of the tilted ski, and the curved side of the ski itself causes it to turn.

Notice the similarity to what we call the "inside-inside move" in racing through a giant slalom, or a NASTAR (National Standard Ski Race) course (*p. 50*). Here the weight on the inside edge of the downhill ski, as we finish the previous turn, is about to be trans-

ferred to the inside edge of the uphill ski, which will become the new turning ski.

Skiing down a mountain, whether in a snowplow turn or in a racing turn, comes back to the same fundamental: the willingness of the skier to commit himself to a complete transfer of weight from ski to ski.

Finding a Comfortable Body Stance

Just as you naturally transfer weight from foot to foot to walk or run, you have a natural body position for standing. Readiness for athletics requires a body stance that is both relaxed and allows you to move quickly from foot to foot as well as shift weight from the ball to the heel of the foot.

A comfortable stance is as important in skiing as in any other sport, and there is no rigidly prescribed position. It varies from individual to individual, depending on body type.

Here is an initial exercise for finding the body stance you feel most comfortable with. Not only is it an exercise we teach to beginners, it also may be used at the beginning of the season by racers to rediscover the feel for their bodies.

Coaches who believe a skier may be having body stance problems also use this exercise, as well as the exercises that follow, to "deprogram" bad habits.

Here Steve is moving in and out of balance on the skis. The exercise is done on a relatively flat area, stationary or moving very slightly. Discovery is by negative and positive feedback. By deliberately getting into awkward body positions we gradually come to feel what is right. Note the similarity of the comfortable body stance, shown in the third figure, to Phil standing without skis on [p. 51].

Lowered and Raised Body Positions: When to Use Them

Skiing is a sport of motion, not of rigidly held body positions. It is also a sport in which we move up and down on the skis, depending on the terrain, the need to turn, and on the speed at which we are skiing.

Try these various body positions to explore the full range of extension and compression of your body as you ski.

Lowering the body does not mean simply bending at the waist, a common misconception for many skiers. It is a full athletic action of the body, including the flexing of the knees.

Lower Body in Response to Speed

If the body is raised at higher speeds the center of gravity remains high and a lack of stability is felt. Lowering the body lowers the center of gravity and increases the skier's feeling of being stable on the snow, more resistant to forces that cause falling.

Here Steve is moving straight down the hill. As his speed increases he lowers his body. Result? His center of gravity drops and he remains stable despite the higher rate of speed.

To do this exercise, start from a stationary position on terrain suitable for straight running. Start slowly and gain speed as you move downhill. As you accelerate, feel the natural desire of the body to drop to a lower position, searching for the most stable running stance.

The same phenomenon should occur in turning. In a turn we raise the body at the beginning to unweight and to release the pressure of the skis on the snow so that we can turn the skis. Toward the end of the turn [*above*] we drop the body and the hip to the inside to counter the centrifugal forces of the turn.

In a turn the body starts down the fall line of the hill and accelerates. As the turn progresses, and speed increases, the body is lowered to create stability.

Deprogramming

Good skiers, from time to time, fall into bad habits. Body positions can get out of kilter, and without the skier being aware of what's wrong. What you see here are exercises not designed for the beginner but for the good skier seeking to regain the right feel for the ski. They are done on one ski, traversing and in straight running.

By exaggerating forward and backward body positions, moving in and out of balance on the ski, we can feel what is awkward and unnatural and what is comfortable and correct.

The modern ski is made in such a way that the skier can find a natural stance centered over the middle of the ski [*center figure opposite page*]. A person who has been skiing too far forward on the ski, for example, will appreciate the need to moderate his body position by trying an exaggerated forward stance on the ski.

We learn right from wrong, and the sensation of awkwardness leads to an acute perception of what is right. In so doing we can deprogram faults in our skiing.

Good skiers should use these exercises to find biases in their skiing. The exercises, not all shown here because of their repetitiveness, are as follows:

Straight Running

Lifting right ski

Lifting left ski

Leaning backward

Leaning forward

Finding most comfortable body position

Traversing

Lifting uphill ski

Lifting downhill ski

Leaning backward

Leaning forward

Finding most comfortable body position

Being able to balance properly over one ski is a foundation stone of modern skiing.

Transferring Weight From One Ski to the Other

To repeat what we said at the beginning of this section, the most common failing of skiers all over the world today is their inability to commit their body weight to one ski.

In traversing, for example, we see this fault in skiers who attempt to cross the hill with their weight on both skis instead of standing on the edged downhill ski.

When conditions are icy the fault may be observed at its worst. The skier slides and skids. Why? Because by traversing with his weight on both skis the skier may have as little as half his body

weight available to apply pressure on the critical uphill edge of the downhill ski. This is the edge that, if weighted abruptly to create maximum pressure, could prevent him from sideslipping down the icy slope.

Practice the simple exercise of standing on the snow and stepping from one ski on to the other. As in walking, note that the weight transfer is total. Shift from one ski to the other, standing independently on each leg. This is the effect you want to create in your skiing.

Now do the same exercise but with a different emphasis. As you traverse across the hill, raise the uphill ski and glide solely on the downhill one. Then place the uphill ski back on the snow. Again, lift it and traverse on the downhill ski. You are now skiing with independent leg action.

In all these exercises emphasize the complete transfer of weight from one ski to the other.

Extending the Leg with Knee and Hip

In the previous exercise we practiced gliding in a traverse on the uphill ski. This is a key move in skiing, and it is made possible by modern skis and boots. What it does is to allow the early initiation of turns on the outside ski.

The correct way to make this move is shown here in detailed pictures of the leg [*opposite page*] and of the overall figure of the skier [*above*]. From a traverse with both knees moderately flexed, we shift all the weight onto the uphill ski *by straightening the knee and hip with an extending upward motion.* The result is to lift the downhill ski off the snow.

The Lateral Step

The ability to move across the hill, acting with independent leg action, is a key building block of ski technique. Let's continue the traverse exercises.

We have learned that by straightening the knee and hip of the uphill leg, the downhill ski becomes totally unweighted. Now we'll do it on an easy slope with more of a lateral move of the uphill leg.

Traversing across the hill, we displace the uphill leg to the side, pushing off the downhill ski. We place the uphill ski on the snow, and then straighten the knee and hip on that side. Again, the effect is to shift the total body weight onto the uphill ski, which continues to glide. Note that the downhill ski is lifted off the snow as a result of the action of the uphill leg straightening.

The same sequence is seen in greater photographic detail of the leg below the hip. Note the complete transfer of weight. The legs move laterally, in a sidestep, when shifting weight. The uphill ski is placed more or less flat on the snow here.

Weight shift, independent leg action, and the lateral step are designed to prepare us for the modern ski turn.

Traversing and Lateral Stepping on Steeper Terrain

Here we are traversing on a steeper slope, and the lateral step has been exaggerated. But the extension of the uphill leg is the same and the downhill ski comes off the snow. Because of the steepness of the hill, the uphill ski does not lie flat on the snow but is edged.

Stepping in this manner, and gliding on the edged uphill ski, we gain a higher line of traverse on the hill. This is a move frequently used by giant slalom skiers to make fine adjustments in their line of descent through gates. The skier's force is channeled sideways.

A variation is the forward lateral step, seen on these pages. We step onto the edged uphill ski at the same time we project it forward. This is an aggressive, accelerating move used by racers, but as a traversing exercise it is entirely within the ability of the recreational skier. Note the scissoring action of the downhill ski. The skier's force is channeled sideways and forward.

Sum-Up

In the past, ski instruction measured progress by ability to perform certain kinds of turns. If you could snowplow, you were a beginner. If you could make a rough, skidded parallel turn, you were an intermediate. If you could short-swing down the fall line of the hill, you were advanced. Progression tended to be measured by the pupil's ability to demonstrate the final forms of ski turns.

Certainly you want to be able to perform these maneuvers on skis, but being able to make a certain kind of turn, if you think about it, is a result of mastering underlying skills. Our approach is to focus on the skills, not their results. They are skills we have learned at the level of World Cup racing, but we believe all skiers have the potential to learn them.

To ski down a mountain we use the same natural body movements employed in walking or running. These movements are

generated by the body, but in skiing—where gravity and speed come into play—they are also influenced by forces outside the body. These forces, nevertheless, can be used in a natural way to help the skier master all kinds of terrain and snow conditions in a comfortable manner.

The first step in integrating the movements of skiing is to allow the skier to feel a natural stance. Many of the exercises we have shown in this section are designed to help you find your most stable and comfortable body position. This is especially important because every human being has a slightly different natural and balanced body position.

The progression also shows how uncomfortable it can feel if exercises are done in the wrong way, thus helping the pupil remember the right way.

These exercises can be practiced at slow speeds, to ensure that weight shift, for example, is taking place correctly. As you master the exercises, increase speed. No progress takes place in learning to ski without increasing speed. With correct technique, speed does not pose the risk of danger.

Many skiers on the slopes today are a risk to themselves and other skiers because they ski fast without proper technique. They ski with what are called "windshield-wiper turns." The skis are thrown around without any emphatic edging, just a general skidding. Consequently there is no precision to their skiing and they cannot truly control their line of descent.

With modern ski equipment there is no excuse for such skiing. As we have demonstrated, the basis of modern skiing is a commitment by the skier to shift weight from ski to ski, to commit the body to a single ski at a time. It is a movement natural to all athletics, made possible today in skiing by the design of the ski and the support of the boot. We will explain these ideas in more detail in Section 2.

TWO IS BETTER THAN ONE

Twenty-seven years before the slalom at Sarajevo, another, more unusual birth was recorded—in Yakima, Washington. Mary Mahre and her husband, Dave—a ski patrolman, fruit grower, and mountain climber—had their fifth and sixth children, born four minutes apart. Phil won that one too.

We were born on May 10, Mother's Day. It was 1957, the year the Brooklyn Dodgers moved to California, Humphrey Bogart died, the Russians launched Sputnik 1, and kids were plugging nickels into jukeboxes to hear "Love Letters in the Sand."

The region of Yakima, where we were born and which we have never wanted to leave after tens of thousands of miles of travel, lies to the east of the Cascades. The mountains to the west scoop up moisture from the Pacific, which falls in mammoth amounts of soft, wet snow—the kind we learned to ski on. By contrast, Yakima is sunny, semiarid country.

We soon moved from Yakima to Ellensburg to live on an orchard that Dad was buying. Our great-grandfather had come to the United States in 1857 from Germany, worked in logging camps, and eventually moved westward. Granddad, his son, came to the Yakima Valley in 1904, settled down, and planted peach and apricot trees.

Occasionally, snow would fall on the orchard, but we didn't really start to ski until we were six years old. Dad had a job as a ski patrolman at White Pass, an eighty-mile drive from Ellensburg.

A view of the Yakima River from Phil's house. It is sunny, dry country, but the snow cascades on the mountains to the west where we grew up.

TOM LIPPERT

When he was away at the ski area, lots seemed to go wrong. Once we drove his tractor into a canal. Another time we decided to help him by pruning the apple trees while he and the other kids were at church. Dad always told us to give whatever we did a hundred percent of our attention, so we pruned two rows of apple trees to knee height.

We swam in an old tank in which they mixed the spray for the trees. We made forts with our older brother and his friend out of apple boxes. When the tractor came to pick them up the whole pile collapsed. Dad told us time and again not to do it. One of the few times he spanked us was when we were about eight years old and had hiked to Lookout Point, overlooking Yakima. We didn't return until late at night. Our parents were worried sick.

Those were difficult days for raising fruit. Dad couldn't make enough of a living from the orchard, so in 1962 he took a full-time job as a mountain manager at White Pass, where he had been a patrolman. We moved from Ellensburg to Gleed. Dad commuted to work every day, a fifty-mile drive each way. He began to take us skiing on weekends.

As tots we were raised in an orchard. Dad was less happy when we drove the tractor into a canal.   MARY MAHRE

It's difficult to remember when we first became aware that we were twins. We simply thought of ourselves as two brothers in a family of nine children. Yet we were constantly together.

We have always thought alike. Someone would ask a question, and we would both start to answer at the same time. At the table we'd suddenly blurt out almost the same words in conversation. If Steve said ten words they would have been the exact same ones Phil used. To some extent we are still that way.

One time, Johnny Buxman, a close friend of ours on the U.S. Ski Team, was helping us build Phil's house. Phil drew his own blueprints, but hadn't shown them to anyone. We were trying to decide what to build next in a wall area. While Johnny stood there the two of us would grunt, "Uh huh. Yeah. Okay." Then Phil walked off. Johnny cried out, "Hey, what did you guys say?"

We were the same in studying a slalom course together. We'd climb twenty gates without saying a word, each knowing that we agreed on the line. Then we'd come to one place and one of us would turn and say, "What do you think?" If it were anyone else, we'd be talking about a problem every third gate.

Our mother, Mary, and Dad, Dave (beaming behind her), set actual examples;
we didn't hear a lot of conversation about what it means to be good.

If there was a trouble spot on a course, and one of us hit it well,
the other knew he would hit it right too. But if it didn't go right, one
would be on the walkie-talkie to the other with a warning to watch
out.

Gemini—the zodiacal sign for twins, which we missed by eleven
days—are said to love speed and talk a lot off the top of their heads.
That describes us well. We competed and yet we helped one another
throughout our careers. We used one another like rungs in a ladder,
to climb higher. Phil: "There always was someone for me to
measure myself against. I would coach Steven to ski better. When
he became better it was harder for me to beat him, and so I got
better.

"In the starting gate I wanted to win, even beat him. But as soon
as I got to the bottom I'd be on the walkie-talkie telling him what he
had to do to beat me."

Twinship may have caused us to view life in the same way, but the
power of our similar thinking really stems from the values forcefully
instilled in us by our parents. Our older brothers and sisters set a

good example too. The Mahre dinner table didn't hear much discussion about what it means to be good. Most of it we picked up by watching. Our parents didn't fight, we never saw them drunk or smoking. We never heard remarks like "You shouldn't do this, but we can do it because we're grown-ups." Even as small children we were treated like adults.

Above all, our father used to insist that "you have to work for what you get. If you want to play football, then practice harder than anyone else. If you set out to do something, do it wholeheartedly, don't go through the motions."

He also said, "Don't be impressed necessarily with what someone else can do. Respect what you see, but never let it beat you. You always do the best you can. Winning isn't everything. It's the effort that counts."

Looking back, it was this attitude, more than anything, that made us different from other racers on the U.S. Ski Team. They could emulate our technique, but often, unfortunately, they couldn't duplicate the attitude.

In 1964 a change took place that would affect the outcome of our lives. The White Pass Ski Area, an abandoned place at night, needed a full-time, resident manager. Nelson Bennett, its director, ordered a house built at the bottom of the mountain, and into it moved the whole Mahre tribe—seven kids, at the time, and our parents. From that moment on, as long as there was snow on the ground—and our season usually lasts for five months—skiing became an everyday part of our lives.

White Pass, even today, is not a giant ski area, but it has fine terrain and has long been a center of racing. The base, where we lived, is at 4,500 feet, and the top of the lifts are at 6,000 feet, for a 1,500-foot vertical—about the same as the Sugar Bowl in California, Mount Snow in Vermont, or Hunter Mountain in New York.

There's no need for snowmaking at White Pass. Snowfall averages eight to twelve feet a winter in the base area. Today the area operates four chair lifts and a couple of drag lifts, and someday it will expand into a former section of the Goat Rocks Wilderness.

Each morning a bus would drive to the Pass to pick up a half

White Pass Ski Area as it appears today. The Mahre house sits at the bottom of the lift (circled). It made skiing an everyday part of our lives.   KEN WHITMIRE

dozen or so Mahre kids and transport us to school. Our mother would have breakfast cooking at 6:30, and we boarded the bus at 7:10. It took almost an hour and a half each way to school, and we used the time to do our homework. Because we were constantly together at other times, the school assigned us to different classes and teachers.

We got home at about five. Mom would have dinner ready, and afterward we would go upstairs to put our ski gear on. Night after night we skied on an illuminated ramp beside the house, climbing it and skiing down. We ran a ten-gate slalom course over and over. All winter long we did that from the age of nine to thirteen. When the skiing was finished in the spring, we used a thick bamboo pole to vault over uprights into the snowbanks.

The first winter we lived at White Pass, Billy Kidd and Jimmy Heuga won their silver and bronze medals at Innsbruck, Austria—

the first ever earned by American men in Olympic Alpine skiing. A couple of winters later, Toni Sailer, the triple gold medal winner at the 1956 Olympics, came to White Pass for the day. He had designed his own fiberglass ski, and we were allowed to ski on a pair. They were too long and too stiff.

We didn't have much money when we were young, and what we did have we had to work for. As we look back we wonder how Dad managed, but there was never a feeling we were poor in any way. We all had hand-me-downs. We wore boots that Mom had used or one of the older kids had outgrown. One winter Phil broke six pairs of wooden skis. It drove Dad crazy. Finally he got smart. He would go to the shop and get a pair of new replacement skis that he would give to Steve. Phil then got the ones Steve had been skiing on. Then when he broke one of those, Dad would pair the remaining ski with one from a previously broken pair.

When that didn't work Dad devised a new solution. He bought what he thought was an indestructible pair of Japanese metal skis with screw-on edges. They lasted almost forever, until Phil rammed them into a bump night-skiing and bent them for good.

By the time we were twelve we began to receive free skis from manufacturers. When we were thirteen—Dad told us years later— he was approached by Rossignol. They asked him if he would sign a contract on our behalf stating that we would use Rossignols for the rest of our careers. He said, "No way!"

We didn't own our first pair of real stretch ski pants until we were fourteen. Up to that time we skied in Levi's. The new pants were black with yellow stripes. We thought we were the hottest-looking things on the hill.

If we bought anything it was usually at ski swaps. To this day we don't care much about dress or how ragged a coat looks.

In the summer we worked for $1.40 an hour so we'd have enough money to pay our race entry fees the following winter. Mom and Dad did what they could for us, but with nine kids it was tough. We ate potatoes often. For meat our parents bought a side of beef at a time and put it in the freezer. Mom was a good cook and our meals (minus some of the vegetables) were as good as any we've ever eaten.

We developed an indifference to luxuries. There was little or no television to influence us. The family didn't have a TV until we were seven, and at White Pass we had to go to the top of the chair lift to get reception.

We were raised unaware of society's frills. Living twenty-five miles from the nearest town, we grew up with limited acquaintances other than family. Perhaps that's the reason why the two of us have grown up as such friends. And without TV we learned to create activities for ourselves.

Occasionally we'd take Dad's ice ax, crampons, ropes, and pitons outside the house and play at mountain climbing. He took us climbing on Mount Rainier when we were seven, and we climbed to the top for the first time when we were fourteen.

There were occasions when Dad would be called to rescue a climber on Rainier. When he came back he'd be so cold that Mom

Dave Mahre is a veteran Everest climber. When we were fourteen, he led us, and friend Bruce Bennett, to the top of Mount Rainier.

would have to start by putting him in a lukewarm bath, then gradually heat up the water to avoid burning him. There were times she must have wondered whether he'd ever come back. But he's tough. That's why, at age fifty-eight, he was back on Everest in 1984 for the second time, climbing with Lou Whittaker.

Mountaineering is not a sport that appeals to us. We've always been interested in speed—motocross, fast water skiing, even trying to race one another up the rope tows at White Pass when we were young.

Dad disciplined the older kids by spanking them, but we can't recall him laying a paddle to us. After raising three older kids our parents realized that corporal punishment didn't accomplish much. They'd punish by scolding us about what we'd done wrong, and why it was wrong. They were always very loving. We never thought once about running away from home.

We were far from being nicely behaved little boys, though. For example, slowing down before we came to a lift line full of people was a lesson we had difficulty learning. When we skied full tilt to the bottom, invariably Dad would catch sight of us. When he did, he'd say, "Let's slow it down before you get here or you're done riding the left for the day."

We also loved the stunt of riding around the bull wheel, a dangerous practice. We'd wait for an empty chair at the unloading ramp on top, then jump on and ride it as the cable wound around the wheel. Dad caught us once and canceled our lift privileges for the whole Christmas holiday. It broke our hearts.

The house at White Pass entailed living at close quarters. We occupied one bedroom. Our oldest brother, Davey, and younger brother Paul slept in another. That left one bedroom for Kathee, Chris, and Jackie, and the bedroom downstairs where Dad and Mom slept. (Our two youngest sisters, Roberta and Ruthie, came later.) There were two bathrooms for all of us. Downstairs there was a living and eating area—small, at least for as many as we were.

Today when the Mahre clan gathers for Thanksgiving or Christmas, we're so many in number that we use the base lodge of the ski area so that everyone can sit and eat together. Including all the

The whole family on skis, Christmas Day, 1968. We're fifth and sixth from the left.

brothers, sisters, our parents, and all our children, we counted thirty at a recent dinner.

Kathee, the oldest, took us in the family car to races. Once we took two days to drive to Mammoth Mountain in California. When we got there Kathee worked as a gatekeeper to earn enough to pay for her food and lodging while we were racing.

Davey, who is seven years older than us and a pilot, was a super slalom skier and an inspiration. But his racing was inconsistent. He might finish two out of ten races in a winter. We'd wait at home for him to return from a race, hoping he'd be carrying a trophy. More often than not he'd trudge in the door and tell us he fell. We would know that taste of defeat later.

Christine, six years older than us, was invited to try out at a U.S. Ski Team training camp. She was a cheerleader and athletic. We were excited. Here was a Mahre almost on the Ski Team! We could do it too. But Chris gave it up. She and Davey were tops academically and went on to college. Our own grades would have qualified us, but by the time we reached our senior year our lives were committed to international racing.

We tried to interest our sister Jackie in racing, but she loved horses and animals. Finally she skied when she was thirteen. A dozen of us hiked up to the top of White Pass, carrying slalom poles. We set a course and tried to coach her. But Jackie started too late to make it to the international ski scene.

Paul Mahre—four years our junior and, at six feet, the tallest of the nine Mahre children—is the only other Mahre to make it all the way to the U.S. Ski Team, that is, to the younger "talent squad." Like Billy Johnson, he's a downhiller, and like Billy he's smart, though not in an academic way, and a little crazy. Billy, for example, can do crossword puzzles seemingly without thinking. Paul loves to read science fiction, and has a kind of "Saturday Night Live" humor. Everything seems funny to him, but then we've always found downhillers slightly crazy. They look at the sport differently.

Paul got into downhill so he wouldn't have to follow our act, a smart move. In high school, though, an incident occurred that caused him to stop skiing. A ski writer, Peter Miller, came to Yakima to interview us. We had heard that Naches High School, where Paul attended school, had a high student dropout rate, but we told Mr. Miller this off the record without checking it. He wrote it anyway. Paul caught hell in school. "If that's what success is all about," he said, ". . . having the press write things you don't want printed . . . I want no part of it." He quit racing for a year, and we didn't want Miller to interview us again.

In his career Paul has been plagued by injuries. In 1983 he jumped over a blind spot on a hill and collided with a Snowcat, breaking his elbow and tailbone. The year before that he broke his ankle in a car accident. Then, in the fall of 1984, just as he was about to get it all together, he tore up his knee in downhill training and had to undergo surgery. At this point he doesn't have too many winters left to prove himself. American racers, including ourselves, usually wind up peaking between the ages of twenty-three and twenty-six.

We twins were always together as youngsters, never apart. We fought only once as kids, when we were eleven. It was a fistfight in our bedroom. We were hitting away at one another when our sister Chris opened the door. "Get out of here!" we shouted. Chris shut the door and we kept at it. Steve recalls that "I hit Phil hard on the nose and he started crying. 'Are you okay?' I asked. Then I started crying because he was crying." It was the last time we fought.

The next winter we were separated for the first time in our lives. Phil had earned a chance to go to the national Jaycee meet for youngsters in Minnesota. Dad escorted him. When they landed at Minneapolis, Phil began to cry and pleaded with Dad, "Let's go home, Dad. If Steve isn't here, it's no good."

Steve remembers his first time alone on the race circuit. "Phil had broken his leg, and I was on the Can-Am circuit by myself. When I wasn't ski racing I'd spend hours working alone on my skis, not socializing with anyone. It was tough not having Phil there."

We are fraternal, not identical, twins, but because of our likeness, people usually assume that we're identicals. Phil has shorter legs and a longer torso, while Steve is an inch taller. Does it make a difference in our skiing? Possibly. The great ski racers over the years, except for downhillers, don't have long legs. Usually they have long trunks and short, stocky legs. Even an inch in leg length can make a difference. The shorter the leg length, the closer the skier's center of gravity to the snow and, accordingly, the greater that person's stability. Steve always has been somewhat more erect in skiing, relying more on hip angulation to edge and pressure the skis in a turn.

Coming out of high school, we each weighed about 140 pounds. When we ended our racing careers we were at 175 pounds plus.

Both of us are vision-impaired, but Steven's eye problems are worse. One way people tell us apart is that Steve often wears glasses. "I had a bad problem of astigmatism, and when I was young I was forced to do special muscle exercises to strengthen one eye. In dry air, particularly, I find contact lenses irritating, so I wear tinted prescription glasses."

At school in Naches, near Yakima, classwork didn't play second fiddle to skiing. As shows more clearly from pictures of that time than now, we're fraternal, not identical, twins.

Eyesight problems didn't limit our skiing. In fact, halfway through the 1984 season Phil quit wearing his contacts. He won his gold medal at Sarajevo without them.

In racing, good peripheral vision isn't necessarily an advantage. In the course itself you need something more like tunnel vision: you don't want to see people at the side of the course, or anything else that may distract you. On the other hand, in recreational skiing, it's a plus to be able to see other skiers coming down the hill and avoid a possible collision.

We got our first contact lenses when we were fifteen. Dad presented them to us. Later we found out it was the folks at the K2 Ski Company who had put up the money to buy them. They also helped to pay for summer courses that allowed us to fulfil our high school course requirements while we were away from home racing in the winter.

Books about twins make the point that one twin is more dominant than the other. There's not much doubt that Phil was the more aggressive one earlier in our careers. It created some difficulties for Steve: "When we were very young, we developed evenly. Phil would win one weekend, I'd win the next. In high school, though,

Even in our teens we were backed by K2 Ski Company. They bought us contact lenses and paid for summer schooling so we could compete in the winter. At left, Bill Kirschner, K2's founder.

he emerged more as the leader. If he wanted to do something, I would follow. I found myself going along with things he wanted to do, even if I might have preferred doing something else. Even in basketball, he would be slightly more aggressive in getting an elbow in. No question, he was the dominant twin back then.

"By the time we reached the level of the national ski team, Phil began to dominate in ski racing too. Increasingly, I began to ask myself, 'Why can't I be doing what Phil is doing?' It didn't help, either, to know that I actually had a year's more experience on the World Cup than he did.

"In 1976, Phil won his first World Cup race—the first international victory for either of us. I thought, 'If he can do it, I can too.' But underneath, I resented that he was the first to break the ice.

"Those were trying times. After all those years growing up together and being so even in racing ability—after training just as hard as Phil did—I didn't make the jump ahead and he did. For the first time I started to hear the words 'Yeah, that's Phil's brother, Steve.'

"The turning point didn't come until the 1981–82 season. That's when I began to experience a new mental toughness, one I hadn't felt before. For the first time I heard myself saying, 'I'm better than Phil.' At the World Championships in Schladming, Austria, Phil had fallen in the first run of the giant slalom. I asked him to come and inspect the second run with me because I respected his knowledge of g.s. more than I respected my own. As we studied the course he talked about the second run just as if he were going to be competing himself. It filled me with confidence. I went on to win the gold medal over Stenmark."

The term "dominant twin" doesn't really describe it. One of us has never tried to dominate the other. According to Phil, "I had more success than Steve at racing because I was more consistent. And consistency is a mental thing—toughness and awareness. I set my sights on becoming the best in the world sooner than Steven did.

"We competed at the same time as we cooperated. If I couldn't win, I hoped my brother would win. If Steven won, it was a victory for me. He was like an extension of me.

"Toward the end of the 1981 season I had to be second or better in a race to win the World Cup over Ingemar Stenmark—to be the first American to win the World Cup—and there were only two more races left to do it in.

"Steve was first out of the starting gate in the first run and was faster than anyone else. Stenmark and I both finished well behind him. Even before the second run started, the European journalists were speculating whether Steve would throw the race to me. They recalled the time, a half-dozen winters before, when Gustavo Thoeni [the Italian who won four World Cups] had a chance to beat Ingemar for the cup in the last race of the season. It was a head-to-head dual slalom. Everyone on the Italian team went into the tank to ensure that Gustavo would win.

"But there was no way Steve was going to let me win, and I would not have appreciated a hollow victory such as Thoeni had gained. Besides, Steve had a chance to place third in the World Cup slalom standings if he raced well. Why should he give that up?

"Steve blasted down the second run, and wound up second to the Russian, Zhirov. I managed to place third but, of course, it wasn't enough to clinch the World Cup. The journalists couldn't understand how my own brother had stood in the way of the first American chance to win the World Cup. Three days later, however, I placed second in a giant slalom race at Laax, Switzerland, and did win the 1981 World Cup."

Essentially, we competed *with* one another, not *against* one another. When you compete with someone you're saying, "If he can do it, I can do it." On the other hand, if you compete against somebody, you're saying, "I'm going to beat him and beat him until he goes down."

When one of us beat the other while competing, the one who lost that day would say, "Well, now I'm going to have to work to be better."

PHASES OF THE TURN

In Section 1 we took a look at some of the basic elements of ski technique. Call them the building blocks of the turn. Paramount among them are:

A comfortable body stance, balanced.
The ability to shift weight in a committed way from one ski to the other.
Up-and-down movement of the body to release and apply pressure of the skis on the snow.

Each of these elements comes into play in the phases of a ski turn.

The poles laid on the snow on page 94 segment the arc of a ski turn into its four phases. We have deliberately shown the phases of the turn, with and without a giant slalom pole, in order to make a point: the turn is the same for a racer as it is for a recreational skier.

Preparation Phase: The first segment of the turn is called "the preparation phase." It marks both the completion of the previous turn and the preparatory phase of the new turn. Or, to put it another way, the end of one turn is the beginning of the next.

Turning down a mountain is a continuous process. The compression of the body, which we saw in Section 1, marking the completion of the turn, pressuring the skis, actually serves as the springboard to start the next turn.

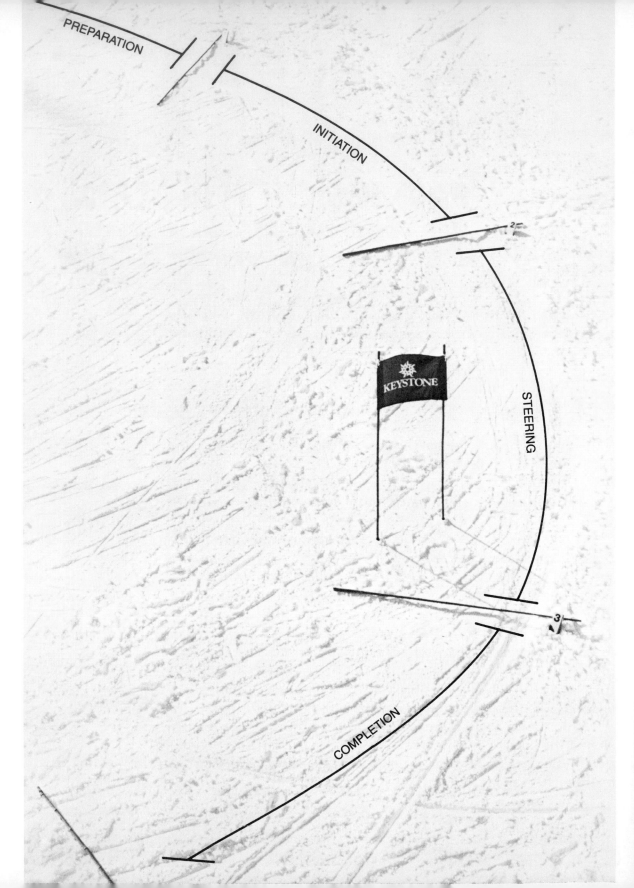

Initiation Phase: In the second phase of the turn we initiate the change of direction of the skis, usually by an up motion that releases the pressure of the skis on the snow, allowing them to be directed in a new path.

Steering Phase: In the third phase of the turn the outside ski is applied to the snow to carve the arc of the turn. Depending on the force applied to the ski, and where applied, the turn may be steered or arced in a smaller or larger radius. The bending properties of the ski, and its curved side profile, create a turning tool.

Completion Phase: The turn is completed to the extent the skier desires. The extent of the completion phase up or down the hill depends on where the skier wants to go in the next turn.

The less completed the turn, the greater the tendency of the skis to go faster and downhill.

A totally completed turn results in an uphill-directed arc that brings the skier to a stop.

Again, the completion phase also marks the preparation for the next turn.

Each phase of the turn calls for distinctive body movements, as demonstrated in Section 1, and each calls for the skier to bring into play distinctive design and mechanical properties of the ski.

How Skis Are Designed to Turn

If you want to make a beautiful object you have to understand and use the tools at hand. If you want to carve a beautiful ski turn you have to understand and use the ski as a tool under your foot.

Looked at one way, ski technique is simply a manual of instruction for how to use a tool called a "ski."

Our success as ski racers was coupled with years of testing new skis. We constantly searched for skis that might cause us to go faster or to turn more easily and quickly. We came to understand the design properties of skis and how to put them to work on the snow.

It is no less important for the recreational skier to understand how and why a ski is designed the way it is. Only by understanding its functions can you explore all the possibilities of ski technique.

Side Cut and Taper Angle: A ski is made with a curved side, called its side cut. The ski is widest at the front end near the shovel, narrowest at the waist under the foot, and then it flares again at the tail, though not usually to its width at the front.

The angle that runs from the widest forward point back to the widest aft point is called the taper angle. The greater that angle, the more the ski is inclined to turn.

The very slightly curved side, however, is not all that causes the ski to turn. If it were, then we would be limited to making giant 100-foot-radius turns.

Side Geometry

Side Cut—The maximum distance from a line drawn between the widest points of the ski and the side of the ski.

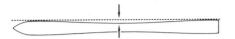

Taper Angle—The angle which runs from the widest forward point backwards to the aft wide point. The taper angle has perhaps more to do with the ski's turn initiation effort than any other design characteristics.

The greater the angle, the easier the ski is to initiate into a turn.

What makes the ski turn more sharply is a combination of the side cut or taper angle and the flex of the ski.

Flex and Camber: A ski is built in such a way that if you lay it on a flat surface it will rest on the tip and tail and be raised in the middle. This is called "camber." When a ski is flexed by downward pressure from the skier, it is said to be "decambered."

The most notable result of decambering a ski is to give the ski more of a curved side. The downward flexing of the ski, together with its side cut, causes the ski to describe a more tightly shaped arc. The more you apply pressure, the more the ski decambers and the tighter the arc of the turn it wants to make.

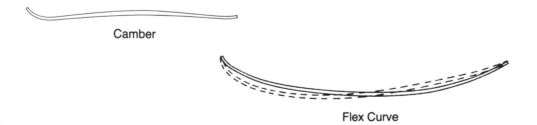

Camber

Flex Curve

This is an important fact to know when you ski. It comes into play in the steering and completion phases of the turn just described.

The two essentials of making a ski turn are to put it on its edge and to decamber it. The more pressure you apply to the ski in the steering and completion phases of the turn, the more it is decambered and the sharper the arc of the turn the ski will make.

Flex Distribution and Torsional Rigidity: Flex distribution is an expression of how a ski distributes your weight on the snow. The flex of a ski also determines how forgiving it will be on difficult terrain and how easily it will move into and out of a turn.

Torsional rigidity is a ski's resistance to twisting from side to side. It's important because it allows you to move quickly from edge to edge, for crisp, controlled turns, even on icy snow. If a ski has too much torsional rigidity, it will be unforgiving and hard to control; if it has too little, it will not hold on hard snow, or will tend to "wash out" in turns.

The foregiveness of a ski is affected by both its stiffness distribution and by its side cut. In soft snow, stiffness tends to dominate, while on hard snow the side cut dominates.

A softer ski generally is easier to initiate into a turn; a stiffer ski will generally track better and will be more stable at higher speeds.

The ability of a ski to hold on ice is affected by both stiffness distribution and by the torsional stiffness of the ski.

Torsional rigidity is a ski's resistance to twisting. If a ski has too little torsional rigidity, it will not hold well on hard snow and ice. It may also tend to wash out in turns. On the other hand, if the ski has too much torsional rigidity, it will be unforgiving and hard to control.

Good torsional rigidity in a ski will allow you to move quickly from edge to edge for crisp, controlled turns.

Damping: For stable skiing it is desirable to have a ski that doesn't vibrate too much in the forebody and the tail. A ski that is well damped does not vibrate. The desired amount of damping varies by type of skiing, speed, terrain, snow, and individual preference. A ski that is too damp is one that will feel dead and unresponsive, and it may run slowly. A ski that is not damped will feel overlively.

Damping—This characteristic is best defined as the ski's ability to feel supple and quiet while it's working through a turn.

Fore and Aft: We have said that you can influence the way a ski turns by pressuring it when it's on edge—that is, by decambering it. The more pressure that is applied, the greater the tendency of the ski to turn.

The willingness of a ski to turn is also affected by whether you pressure it in front or behind. The more you pressure the forebody of the edged ski in a traverse, for example, the more the ski will want to turn up the hill. On the other hand, pressuring the edged tail of the ski will cause little turning action.

Fore and aft pressure on the ski is also related to "slow" and "fast" in skiing. Pressuring the front of the ski is a slowing action; pressuring the tail of the ski is an accelerating action.

Learning all about the properties of your skis and how they affect your skiing clearly helps you improve your skiing. Skiers who haven't taken the trouble to learn how a ski works will be limited in their progress. Skiers with a good knowledge of equipment can explore the many different ways skis can help them ski better.

Armed with the knowledge of how a ski turns, you are ready to understand the dynamics of the turn itself.

Turn with Up and Down Motion

We are now going to bring together some of the elements, or building blocks, discussed so far. Among the most important is a good up-and-down action by the skier.

The skier on opposite page exhibits a lack of up-and-down action, which, unfortunately, is the case with many recreational skiers today. Note that in changing direction he fails to flex his legs. As a result his skis skid haphazardly across the snow. He is never able to transfer weight definitively to the outside ski, and the inside ski of the turn is dragged around.

Note the very definitive up-and-down action of Steve [*pp. 102-3*] as he performs a simple turn on the outside ski.

"In the completion phase of the turn, my body is lowered partly as a result of the compressive forces of completing the previous turn.

"I rise in the *preparation* phase of the turn and step onto the uphill ski, which will become the outside turning ski of the new turn. My upward extending motion releases pressure of the skis on the snow and permits me to begin the turn. This is the *initiation*

phase. The straightening of the uphill leg and hip raises the downhill ski off the snow, which also signals a complete transfer of my weight onto the outside ski.

"In the third and fourth figures I am in the *steering* phase of the turn. I begin again to lower my body as downhill speed and compressive forces come into play in the turn. My lowered center of gravity also supplies stability.

"In the completion phase of the turn my knees and hips reach their point of greatest flexion. From totally up in the initiation phase, I have come to all the way down in the *completion* phase of the turn. Note also how the pressure of my body weight and the momentum supplied by my speed have caused the ski to decamber in a pronounced arc, causing it to turn."

Steering and Completion

The steering and completion phases of a ski turn are clearly seen in the sequence of photos on these pages. They are accompanied by a pronounced down motion.

Note the four key elements of technique in these two phases:

The inside edge of the outside turning ski is in a bending arc created by the side cut of the ski and decambering. Consequently, the radius of the turn is being tightened.

The edge is pressurized by a total commitment of the skier's body to the ski.

The lower body position—hence lower center of gravity—enables the skier to find stability.

The skier is building forces that will kick into the preparatory phase of the next turn.

There are no prescribed body positions in skiing, only motion. From the motion, certain body positions may appear.

Finding a Balanced Position on the Ski

Since the modern ski turn is made essentially on one ski—and a series of linked turns by moving from one ski to the other—it is critical that the skier be able to balance properly on a single ski. This is not as hard as it sounds. First, the materials and engineering in modern ski manufacturing have resulted in a ski that you can maneuver from a comfortable, upright, neutral body position, centered on the middle of the ski. Higher, rigid plastic boots offer plenty of support for the skier's balance too.

Second, we have created exercises to develop your ability to balance on a single ski, one at a time, as you traverse and turn.

Here we are traversing the hill standing on one ski. Steve finds his balance on the ball and heel of the foot. Notice his body position in the first figure at left, how upright and natural it is.

The second group of pictures shows the skier going in and out of balance when turning; these are exercises for advanced skiers.

Again, we can create an out-of-balance feeling either by using an exaggerated forward body position or by leaning backward on the ski.

The exercises here move the skier forward and back on the ski, so that he can gradually find a centered position [*below*] where he feels most comfortable.

One-pole and No-pole Exercises for Balance

Finding the right balance position on the ski is best done without the distraction of poles as a prop. Ski poles should be used for other purposes, such as a trigger to start the timing of the turn, to supply rhythm to the turn, and for recovery. But not for balancing.

Here the turn is done on the outside ski without poles. Again, notice the centered position of the skier on the ski.

You can also do these exercises with one pole. Many people have a tendency to turn more easily in one direction than another, and taking away the pole on one's weaker side removes the crutch effect and forces the skier to balance properly on the turning ski in a manner that will eventually cure weak-sided turning.

The exercise is also done on the inside ski. It is even more difficult to turn on the inside ski if your weight is not precisely centered on the ski. Turning on the inside ski forces the skier to feel out the perfect balanced position for skiing.

We do exercises on the inside ski for two added purposes. First, because it is so much more difficult to turn on the inside ski, doing it serves to remind us of the ease and efficiency of steering on the outside ski at all times. Second, there are actually situations when the inside ski *is* used in a turn, as we shall see in Section 3, on the White Pass Turn.

Linked Turns, Footwork, and the Outside Ski

As we develop the capacity to balance on one ski, we perfect our ability to move easily from ski to ski, carving precisely on the outside ski of each turn.

Here we see a simply executed form of the modern ski turn as it becomes linked in a series down the hill. There is nothing fancy here, only basics. Steve performs: "I start at the top, steering on the

outside ski [right leg]. In the second figure I am completing the turn on the inside edge of the ski. Next I step onto the other foot. I commit my weight to the outside ski of the new turn, carving on its inside edge. This is sometimes called the inside-inside move, because I am going from the inside edge of one turning ski to the inside edge of the other.

(Sequence continued on page 117)

"In the figure at the extreme right [*opposite page*] my outside ski is carving hard on the snow. I complete the turn on the left foot and prepare to step on to the right ski to start the next turn."

The ease with which the turn is done is a reflection of the almost perfect balance, or centering, of the skier on the turning ski.

The Feel-bad Turn

If it's true that you won't do what's good for you unless you know what's bad, then this is the turn that proves that adage in skiing.

The aim here is to get you to make a turn on the inside ski. Of course you're supposed to make the turn on the outside ski, but until you can feel all the things that go wrong when you turn on the inside (incorrect) ski, you'll never appreciate the importance of getting all your weight and turning pressure on the outside ski when you turn.

To turn on the inside ski, lean in and find your balance on the edge of the ski. Pressure the ski forward and on the edge to make the arced side of the ski want to turn on the snow, and then feel yourself come around.

Note how the inability to angle your upper body in relation to your legs causes a feeling of instability. If the snow is at all icy, your edge will slip because your unstable body position prevents you from putting adequate pressure on the edge of the turning ski. None of this would be the case if you were turning on the outside ski.

Making a number of linked turns on the inside ski is not only tiring, it's like hitting your head with a hammer. It feels good when you stop. One positive lesson, though: to ski on the inside ski, you must be centered on the ski to make it turn. It you are forward or back on the ski, it won't turn properly.

The Feel-good, Feel-bad Turn

Steve continues: "This is also known as doing a series of linked turns, all on the same leg. In this case I am turning continuously on my right leg. As a result my leg is on the outside ski in the first turn, and on the inside ski in the second turn . . . and so on. It's like doing a series of right and wrong turns, and the feeling for the importance of skiing correctly, which it generates, is powerful.

"Note in the first turn the solid balance inherent in my skiing as I'm able to plant the pole downhill and angulate my body. As I stay on the right ski to make the second turn, I must tilt my body to the inside and try to hold my balance on the ski. The slightest irregularity in the terrain will throw me off.

"Going from easy to hard turns by remaining on the same ski is an exercise for better skiers. It creates a fresh awareness of the importance of independent leg action in skiing and the need to pressure the outside ski of the turn.

"It also shows that it is possible to initiate a turn on the inside ski."

Turn with Hop Motion

Here is an exercise to enhance your progress toward strong independent leg action.

Earlier in this section we noted that the initiation phase of the turn is characterized by a straightening of the leg and hip—a lightening of the pressure of the skis on the snow—to start the turn in a new direction.

Here the up motion is exaggerated to a hop. Both skis are lifted off the snow. With total unweighting it is possible to pivot the skis effortlessly into the new turn.

However, this is not a jump-and-land-on-both-skis exercise. Note that in the third figure Phil is preparing to land on the outside ski of the new turn. The touchdown on the snow is accompanied by a flexing of the knee to absorb the shock.

Perfect balance on the outside ski makes the touchdown easy, and the ski—decambered and its edge pressured on the snow—continues to arc the turn through the steering and completion phases.

Sum-Up

In this section we have presented some vital lessons about the modern ski turn—lessons that have been passed on from the highest levels of international racing to practical application in recreational skiing.

There are four phases to the turn: preparatory, initiation, steering, and completion. These four phases occur in recreational turns as well as in racing turns.

The ski is engineered to enable you to carry out each phase of the turn as efficiently as possible. If you understand how the ski is designed, you will be able to put it to work for you in improving your turning technique.

Because modern technique calls for the turn to be executed on one ski, it is necessary to practice exercises that will enable you to find a comfortable, balanced position on the ski. Turns done on the inside ski force the skier to find a centered position on the ski in order to make it turn.

A correct turn is steered and finished on the outside ski. This is the easiest and most efficient way to turn. The difficulties of attempting to steer on the inside ski of the turn dramatize the difference.

If you are an accomplished skier but want to improve your ski technique further, practice these exercises whenever you can. All the time you practice you are improving your capacity for independent leg action, the cornerstone of modern ski technique.

THREE

HOW TO GROW YOUNG SKI CHAMPIONS

Phil won his first ski race at the age of nine on Easter Sunday, April 11, 1965. It was a small fry slalom at Stevens Pass, a ski area north of Yakima, in the Wenatchee National Forest. Steve came in second. Mom said it happened that way because it was the order in which we were born. The next year it was the other way around: Steamer was first and Beamer—that's what our Dad called us—was second. The competition had started.

We first raced in the Mighty Mite League, which later became the Buddy Werner League. Everyone raced together. Kids from Yakima, Seattle, and Tacoma competed against one another as Red, Blue, and Yellow teams. You stayed with your team for the whole winter.

We loved that form of competition. The organizers kept the two of us on separate teams so it wouldn't be unfair for the other kids.

That experience of team skiing stuck with us through our careers. Even on the U.S. Ski Team we appreciated that while ski racing is an individual sport, in training it's a team sport. You learn to help your teammates and to put up gates for the others to ski through.

Steve recalls that "I would try to get the guys on my team to go fast. Phil would try to get his team to ski faster. We used to say, 'Hey, there's no hill too fast for us.' "

The races revolved around team challenges. The times of all the racers on a team were totaled to determine the winner for the week. So you had to work with other kids as well as yourself. But when you went down the hill, it was individual. Just like it would be for us on the U.S. Ski Team.

What is the right age to start a kid ski racing? It's hard to think of anyone who eventually has made the U.S. Ski Team who didn't start skiing before they were ten years old. Starting at the age of five would be the best.

Kids up to twelve or thirteen years of age should not ski in a strictly coached environment. Ski racing should be fun. When it's done as team competition, as we learned it, everyone is in it together.

The first priority is that kids learn to ski as fast as they can. That may sound a bit frightening to parents, but speed is relative. Our parents have always skied conservatively, but there was a time when we twins had to go all out to keep up with them. We thought they were going really fast.

A youngster normally will only go up to a speed he or she feels comfortable with, anyway. Some kids are never going to have as much racing potential as others because their comfort zone is different. Speed feels scary to them, and they won't let themselves go fast.

Parents who are concerned about allowing their kids to ski fast should consider the fact that the youngster probably runs a greater risk of being hit by a car in front of the house than of breaking a leg skiing. We used to ski through the woods as fast as we could. If Dad had seen what we were doing, he probably would just have shaken his head or told us to get back on the patrolled, open slope. He knew how crazily we were capable of skiing. He simply thought it was the best way for us to learn. His attitude was, "If you get injured, maybe you won't ski as fast the next time."

Youngsters who start to ski at the age of five have a head start. Steve thought it was a good idea when he was three.

A youngster can no more be coached to ski fast than he can be taught to overcome the fear of height. How do you stop a kid from unconsciously tightening his grip on the safety bar of the chair lift? You can't, any more than you can force him to overcome a fear of speed. On the other hand, if a kid has a desire for speed, it should take precedence over learning technique.

A youngster who's constantly taught angulation, and how to keep pressure on the turning ski all the time, will never learn how to let his skis go. On the other hand, if he instinctively learns how to let his skis go—to "bomb the hill"—he will eventually learn how to get his skiing under control with technique.

Speed comes before technique if a youngster is going to succeed in ski racing. Sooner or later he'll learn how to slow down, and a coach can build proper technique on that. What the coach can't teach is speed.

Part of skiing has to be subconscious, like walking. You shouldn't have to think about it. That's why there's no substitute for a youngster getting his or her miles on skis. Literally, hundreds of miles. Kids have to feel their skis become extensions of their feet.

The comparison of walking and skiing is meaningful. When you walk there is both an unconscious part to the act and a conscious part. You can walk unconsciously, but when you come to the corner you have to think about making a turn. The same is true of skiing. The body movements to make the turn have to be unconscious so that you can concentrate on when and where to make the turn.

Of course a youngster will develop incorrect moves on skis that become unconscious. They have to be deprogrammed later. When he first saw Steve skiing, our coach, Harald Schoenhaar, remarked that Steve was extending his hand too far out to the side. He was planting his pole two or three times in a turn. It felt very aggressive, but all it was doing was interrupting the natural body movements. It was wasting energy in the upper body. So the coach corrected the error. An unconscious habit had been brought to light—and corrected.

But all of that should come later in a youngster's upbringing on skis. We didn't undergo any close coaching until we were in our mid-teens.

First, a youngster has to learn to ski fast. Then he must acquire a technique to bring the speed under control. Finally, good coaching will refine that technique, and make the kid use it to go still faster.

The wrong way is to teach a kid a totally refined technique before he has developed his own potential to go fast.

Overcoaching youngsters is a tragic mistake. You see it in football today. Little ten-year-olds are being coached as if they were being prepared for the NFL. The coach is sending in plays from the sideline. He puts them in a pro set—a wide receiver out, the back in motion, double tight end. The kids are made to learn ten plays and four formations for each. Good God, it's all too complicated for youngsters of that age. They're not able mentally to cope with that kind of complexity *and* the physical skills of playing.

As youngsters we competed on opposing teams. At this age, heavy technique coaching should be avoided. Concentrate on going fast.

Similarly, in skiing, too much coaching and technical complexity can hurt a kid. Teaching formal ski school movements results in the kid learning skills to keep speed in check when, in reality, the young racer needs to learn how to maximize speed.

In the end the key to success for a youngster is to amass a huge number of miles on skis, coupled with a raw desire to go as fast as possible. That will count for more than any amount of coaching at a young age. Go as fast as the hill—and faster.

Our first real coaching came from several French ex-racers who were teaching skiing in the White Pass Ski School: Lou Lou Kneubuhler, Loic David, Alain Ronchail, and others. We were eleven, and they worked with us informally for an hour on Saturday and another hour on Sunday. Instead of going to lunch between their scheduled classes, they came on the hill to give us a few pointers. They told us to stand up more when the terrain is flat, to go straighter in gaining speed, and to stay off the tails of our skis. They gave us easy-to-follow tips, not complex instructions about angulating or developing a sophisticated hand position. The Frenchmen, who had seen all of the top racers in Europe, told the people at White Pass that we were as good as any youngster skiing in the Alps at the time.

In addition to skiing every weekend, we practiced every night after school by the light of a mercury vapor lamp on the ramp outside the house. That nightly practice paid off. In later years, after we were winning on the World Cup, the experts who were struggling to find a formula to develop a broad base of talented young racers in America concluded that maybe the answer was simply to install a lot of families at the base of a mountain, like the Mahres, and get them to raise their children there.

Advantageous as it was for us to grow up at a ski area, nevertheless we think it's possible—though perhaps not likely—for a kid to ski only on weekends and eventually make the U.S. Ski Team. It's a matter of concentration. If the kid will ski for six hours solid each day, it's possible. It won't happen if he just goes out and makes two or three runs, then comes into the base lodge because he's cold. When we were kids it didn't matter what the conditions were on the mountain or how cold it was. We were out there skiing. The kid who's prepared to ski in all kinds of snow and weather is the one who will make it.

A kid has to be willing to make sacrifices. Concentration and drive count most. We hated summer training, and we never did much running or other physical conditioning. For us the best conditioning for ski racing was skiing. No other sport quite develops the muscles you need for alpine skiing.

People often assumed that we were lazy about training, that we made it on sheer talent. They didn't know our secret: the concentration we put into our skiing when we did train. Tom Kelly, a coach on the U.S. Ski Team for many years, once said of us, "They're workhorses. They don't train much in summer, but when they train, they put more into it—and get more out of it—than anybody else. They go full blast."

On the day of a race, for example, the other teams would wait for the lifts to open before they went up. We used to climb with the coaches and set flags for pre-race training. By the time the others showed up, the poles were broken and we had the hill in a regular mess. The early start psyched us up.

We first dreamed of going to the Olympics when we were twelve. Bob Beattie, the U.S. Ski Team director at the time, invited a bunch of small fry to come to a team training camp. The idea was to expose twelve-year-olds to the best racers in the country and ski alongside them. Phil doesn't remember being that impressed: "Those guys didn't seem that good. I didn't come home saying, 'Uh huh, I have a lot of work to do now.'

"I didn't have any role models in skiing I particularly wanted to copy. Sure, I admired Jean-Claude Killy for winning three gold medals, but I didn't want to be like him. Though I've signed thousands of autographs in my life, I've never asked for anyone's autograph. I've never put anyone on a pedestal or thought anyone was necessarily better than me.

"Perhaps I was different because at the age of thirteen I was already one of the best skiers in the Pacific Northwest, beating guys sixteen and seventeen years old.

"We competed in the Buddy Werner League as kids, but the legend of Buddy Werner as a person and famous ski racer didn't mean that much to me, even after I discovered that the league was named for him as a memorial, after he died in an avalanche in Europe. The only personal knowledge I had of him was when I went to see the movie *Other Side of the Mountain*. The way he was portrayed in the movie, I was completely turned off by the guy. But maybe he wasn't like that in real life."

Our parents didn't push us or any of our brothers and sisters to ski. Dad acknowledges that he did little to help us because he was too busy working on the mountain.

Parental pressure to ski does little to help, anyway. A youngster

Buddy Werner gave his name to the league in which we competed.

UPI INT'L

should want to go skiing. Or the parent can suggest going skiing, but definitely leave the decision to the kid. And even when he or she decides to go, there's still the all-important matter of how many miles the youngster is willing to ski.

Before we moved to White Pass, Dad was able to take us skiing only on weekends. We took a brown-bag lunch, and everyone in the family went. We loved it so much, we skied from the moment we got out of the car until it was dark and the lifts shut down.

Racing is the child's decision to make. If he or she really wants to do it, then the parents should back the decision a hundred percent. But parental pressure to ski won't work.

When we were youngsters the national Jaycee organization sponsored an annual Junior Ski Meet and paid the way for scores of kids to attend. We competed in three or four of the Jaycee meets over the years. Some officials at first criticized the idea because they feared it might artificially raise the expectations of youngsters or prematurely put pressure on them. But we like the idea, just as we think the Junior Olympics are fine too.

National events allow a youngster—along with development coaches looking for future prospects for the U.S. Ski Team—to see how good he is. While we knew we were best in our region's age group, we wanted to know how good we were relative to kids from other parts of the country. Those meets helped to raise our sights. We had beaten everyone in our neighborhood; now it was time to go one better.

Phil went to his first national Jaycee meet at Duluth, Minnesota, when he was nine years old, in the company of eight other kids from the state of Washington. Dad took him on the plane, and after the first crisis of a tearful Phil feeling his brother's first absence, things went fine. This was the account Phil gave to the Yakima paper when he got back:

"My Dad and I left Yakima on Friday morning and flew to Spokane and on to Minneapolis. Then we got on a Convair 440 and flew to Duluth, where we found our luggage. Two men took us to the Edgewater Motel.

"We changed into our ski clothes and went to the ski area to look at the race course. The temperature was 18 below zero. Then we went back to the motel and went to bed.

"The next morning we went to the ski area. It was 20 degrees below zero. We took our skis out of the bus. Then the team went to the state flag, and we marched to the award stand. 'The Star-Spangled Banner' was played, a torch was lit, a cannon went off, and a thousand balloons went up in the sky.

"Then we put on our skis and went up the T-bar. Then it was my turn. My ski pole got stuck in a crack. I made it down in 34.73 seconds. My second run I made it down in 34.11 seconds. They gave me a rerun, and I made it down in 34 seconds. Then I got my medal for third place. We went back to the motel. We went to dinner, then I went swimming. The next morning we watched the jumping and cross-country. *Zoom!* I was home."

"The Jaycee meets were a big thing for kids," Phil says now. "They should be revived. I never got an inflated ego by going to one, or thought of myself as Jean-Claude Killy because I had been there."

The last Jaycee meet we entered was at Winter Park, Colorado.

Steve won the slalom, and Phil won the giant slalom. It's never totally fair to compare a competitor's time with the unofficial forerunner's time, but Phil at the age of thirteen had a faster time than Stein Eriksen, who foreran the course.

That was the year, too, when we began to compete in the U.S. Junior Nationals. Phil recalls, "I was skiing in Lange pro boots, which I'd bought at a sale, and blue jeans. I never had a chance to inspect the course for the first run of the slalom because I was standing in the lift line at the bottom, too shy to ask whether I was allowed to cut to the head of the line—which, as a racer, I could have done.

"When I finally reached the top I rushed to the starting gate. The coach said, 'Look ahead!' I missed a sharp turn, straddled a pole, climbed back up so my feet passed through the gate, and made it to the bottom. In the second run I recorded the fastest time in my age group and the second fastest for the field."

We also competed annually in the Spring Series. It was an end-of-season series of races that started in Washington and moved down to Mount Hood in Oregon and to Mammoth Mountain in California and Mount Rose in Nevada. The racers accumulated points, and the whole U.S. Ski Team usually competed. We were thirteen when we first competed, starting from sixtieth position or worse on rutted courses. Occasionally we finished in the first ten. Good as that seemed, our results didn't appear to attract the attention of the U.S. Ski Team. On the other hand, Sheila McKinney, who also was thirteen, was named to the team talent squad. We wondered if it helped to be a girl to make the team.

Over the years the United States consistently has produced more internationally competitive women ski racers than men, and it all starts at a young age. The fact that girls mature and reach their potential earlier is part of it, though that's true for all nationalities, not just American girls.

In America the woman athlete has a far more limited choice of sports she can enter than does a male. She can choose, for example, from volleyball or gymnastics or swimming. And she can pick skiing, which is appealing to the parents because they can share in it as participants. But that's about all.

A young American male, on the other hand, has opportunities facing him in all kinds of major sports: football, baseball, basketball, hockey. As a matter of fact, we loved football and played it in high school. But we were too small to have any kind of future in college ball. In our senior year of high school we still weighed only 140 pounds, and by that time competition and training for ski racing were eating more and more into our late fall schedule.

Still, if everything had been right, and we had lived in town rather than at a ski area, we would have wound up playing football, not skiing.

Doug Flutie, the former Boston College player, and now pro quarterback, is a star competitor who isn't a big guy, but he aspired to football anyway. He is such a standout athlete that there's not much doubt he'd have made it in a number of sports. But for sure we'll never see him as a ski racer. American skiing loses a lot of true male athletes to other sports.

So the superior achievements of American girl skiers over the years—Andy Mead Lawrence, Kiki Cutter, the Cochran sisters—has to be viewed relatively. In comparison with their male peers, they had fewer sports to choose from. And that's how it's bound to continue in America: inherently, more good girl athletes are attracted to skiing.

Europe obviously has produced great woman ski racers, but it has generated an equal—or greater—number of male champions. The reason, again, has to do with the attraction of other sports. In Europe—for a boy—soccer and ski racing are major sports, whereas they are not in the United States. In Europe—particularly in the Alpine countries like Switzerland and Austria—if you're a top ski racer, you're a hero. In the United States skiing is about the last thing a boy will choose if he has the ambition to be a sports hero in high school or college. He'll choose football, basketball, even tennis first. His list of options can go on and on before it ever reaches skiing.

Europe has another advantage over the United States in attracting young athletes to skiing. Almost all the major countries—France, Germany, Austria, Switzerland, Yugoslavia, as well as little Liechtenstein—have mountains. A big part of their populations live near snow and skiing.

In the United States, by contrast, only a relatively small number of people live near skiable mountains. And those who do are in relatively sparsely populated states like Vermont, Colorado, Montana, and Wyoming. And unless a kid comes from ski country, or lives near it, he really doesn't have much of a chance to become a really good skier, let alone a top racer.

The U.S. Ski Team will always have to draw its talent from kids who live in ski country. It's hard to see racers coming from the Bronx or downtown Chicago, or even from affluent suburbs like Scarsdale, New York, Evanston, Illinois, or Scottsdale, Arizona.

Recently we saw an article about two kids from Texas racing NASTAR, the National Standard Ski Race. They were a boy and a girl, eleven and twelve. They were dynamite. They really wanted to become ski racers. And maybe they can, because their parents are well-to-do, own a house in Colorado, and can live and ski there. But that's quite a commitment for a family from Texas to make.

A kid shouldn't be encouraged to think he can be a ski racer—let alone the best—if he can't practice almost every day. Ambitious young tennis players have to get out and hit tennis balls on a daily basis. Our equivalent was skiing in the back of the house, running flags night after night. Any sport has to be pursued with intensity, and few opportunities exist in America for talented young athletes to do that with skiing.

One solution, of course, is to send a kid to a ski academy. There are quite a few of them now, spread about the country, at Burke Mountain and at Stratton, Vermont, and Mammoth Mountain, California, for example. The idea is to allow a kid to pursue a good high school education in a curriculum timetable that allows plenty of ski-race training during the day.

Despite the fact that quite a few skiers on the U.S. Team have come out of ski academies, we're not much impressed with the academies' overall results. They've often produced graduates who had no real racing success because they OD'd on gate skiing.

There are two problems, we think, with ski academies. First is our suspicion that they're a convenience for parents who don't want to, or can't, be involved in their kids' upbringing. The parents are saying, in effect, "Go away to this academy and let it take the responsibility for your development." But we believe that when a kid is in his mid-teens, family life and the role of the parent are very important. Better they should have the guidance of their parents than rely on the influence of their peers.

Academies can't substitute for a parent who's able to supply the child with a notion of what's right and what's wrong, and where skiing is supposed to fit into his life. They do allow a kid to ski a lot and graduate from school, and that's good. Every ski racer should finish high school. Even though we were away almost the entire winters of our junior and senior years, we took summer courses and graduated, in cap and gown, with our class.

The other problem with ski academies is that they take kids in their mid-teens and put too much emphasis on technique. It may be right for some kids, but it's counterproductive in the case of youngsters who have never learned to ski fast. Instead of learning speed and how to go faster, they get a heavy course in technique.

Young people with a talent for ski racing face a tough decision. On the one hand, they must be reminded that only a very few ever make it to the top in ski racing, and that completing their education is vitally important. On the other hand, if they don't become totally involved in ski racing by the age of seventeen, their chance to succeed in skiing won't ever come again. The solution that often suggests itself to many kids and parents is to give ski racing a shot and, if it doesn't work, complete their educations later. Unfortunately, in practice, not many go back to school.

Parents need to involve themselves in a dialogue with their kids about these difficult decisions. What role should education play in their lives? What role skiing? Parent and child need to participate together in resolving these questions.

However, and this is a big "however," no youngster—or parent or coach—should ever encourage the goal of winning an Olympic gold medal. We know from firsthand experience how difficult and chancy it is to realize such a goal, and we've seen the terrible consequences of allowing a kid to think about winning an Olympic medal and then failing.

For the same reason, the idea of instituting a national program to create medal winners—isolating talent squads away from home as they do in Eastern Europe—seems wrong to us. Family life is too important.

It would be nice to think that coaches could pick out talented young ski racers when they're thirteen years old and develop them all the way to the Olympic team, but that hardly ever happens in real life. Some kids peak very early, then level off and go nowhere. Others show no early promise, then suddenly blossom. About the only thing a coach can do is to understand whether the youngster is interested in skiing so that he can hold the kid's attention.

David Kong, born of Chinese parents, is a very talented young ski racer. He went to a ski academy, and coaches who've seen him ski in California have heralded him as another Mahre. Whether David will make it or not is impossible to predict. As we see it, there's a large danger that overcoaching will kill his appetite to go faster and faster.

U.S. Ski Team racer Alan Lauba, when he was twelve or thirteen, had unbelievable technique, he skied so much better than the others his age. But by the time he reached his twenties Alan was no longer skiing well in slalom and giant slalom. And so he switched to downhill. He has even beaten Bill Johnson in training. What caused him to develop this way? What makes a ski racer click?

It's true that we set our sights on skiing in the Olympics when we were twelve, but nothing exceptional was done for us. Our parents devoted no more attention to us than to the other seven kids in the family. We were expected to do well in school, we ranked in the top ten academically in our class, and we played football.

At the same time, at fifteen years of age, we were already faster than some of the seasoned racers on the U.S. Ski Team. The pressure to ski race became greater. But our parents—and we—

Steve, with two medals, and Phil, with one,
flank proud coach Alain Ronchail
after the 1970 national Jaycee meet.

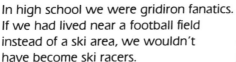

In high school we were gridiron fanatics.
If we had lived near a football field
instead of a ski area, we wouldn't
have become ski racers.

determined that we wouldn't drop out of school. In fact, we liked school. Oddly enough, there were times when we found it more of a sacrifice to ski race than to attend school.

In the spring of 1973 we were racing for the third time in the Spring Series on the West Coast. It was our only real chance to compete against racers on the U.S. Ski Team because we couldn't afford to travel the more extensive Can-Am circuit. We raced well. Phil won the overall title based on cumulative points. Later that summer, he was named to the U.S. Ski Team, realizing a dream. The following year, Steve also made the team.

That fall of 1973, Phil trained with the ski team, then returned home to White Pass. He was supposed to leave for Europe in three days time, but something happened to change his plans. Phil recalls:

"On November 24, for the first time in the season, they opened the lift to the top at White Pass. Five feet of new snow lay on the hill. Steven and I were riding up the chair lift and had almost reached the top when we saw Russ Forman, our sister Kathee's date at the time—and our future brother-in-law. We shouted at Russ, 'Wait, we'll catch up with you.'

"Russ stopped at the head of a very steep pitch on the top of Execution Run to wait for us. We unloaded at the top of the lift and began to ski down toward him. The fresh, deep powder felt wonderful and we didn't want to stop. I cruised over the top of Execution and down the pitch, making first tracks on the face. Steven skied across the face, behind me. Suddenly the snow broke open in a huge fracture line below his feet.

"He yelled down, 'Avalanche!' but it was too late. I could already feel the snow dragging me down. I twisted around, and below me I saw another fracture open in the snow.

"Now Execution actually was sliding above and below me. It was dragging me down and down. I struggled to ski to the left in an attempt to get myself out of the sliding snow. Instead, I twisted out of one ski. Then the snow mowed me down from behind.

"The last thing I saw was a big tree, three or four feet in diameter. I thought to myself, 'I'm going to be dragged down and pinned against the tree, buried, and that will be the end of me.' But it didn't happen. I kept sliding down into the woods. I was concentrating on one thought—'Swim. Stay on top.' But the snow kept rolling over me.

"I didn't know which direction was up or down. In five or six seconds the avalanche had carried me down a couple of hundred feet of open slope, then 250 feet through the trees. Finally, I stopped. I couldn't see a thing. The snow still swirled around my head. I was in a cloud of white. 'Is this heaven, or what?' I wondered.

"I could hear Steven's voice calling from a distance. 'Are you okay?' I hollered back, 'I'm here.'

"I was buried to my waist. I looked back up the hill a short distance and saw the stump of a tree. I must have hit it. My right leg was lying on top of the snow, my left was buried. By the time Steven skied down to where I was lying, my right foot was going numb. I tried to lift up the leg, but the foot stayed on the snow. I knew it was broken, but I felt no pain.

"Russ skied to the bottom of the mountain to fetch a toboggan. He threw it in a Snowcat and drove to where I lay below the stump. They put me on the toboggan. I insisted that Steve take me down. At the bottom they got me into a car and we drove to the hospital in Yakima.

"At the hospital the X rays showed two bones in my leg were broken, at the boot top. It was the end of November 1973, and the season was over. I wouldn't ski again for another year and a half."

3

THE TECHNIQUES OF TURNING

The good skier of the 1980s is easy to spot on the hill. He or she is usually seen turning on the outside ski, with the inside ski often visibly lifted off the snow. Such a skier demonstrates independence of leg action in changing direction on the hill and the ability to balance on a single turning ski.

Another characteristic of today's good skier is a fluid up-and-down action of the body in the turn. The turn is started in the preparation and initiation phases on the balls of the feet. Then, as the turn progresses and crosses the fall line, the good skier increasingly pressures the tails of the skis by shifting weight to his heels.

The fault of most skiers today is that they ski constantly on their heels, or they start the turn on the balls of the feet and finish it on the balls of the feet. They lack the knowledge of how to move back and forth on the ski to make use of its design and materials.

The steering and completion phases of different ski turns vary with the amount and placement—fore and aft—of pressure on the skis.

Another important difference of technique is in the way the skier prepares and initiates the turn. This is what we will show in Section 3, first with traverse exercises, then with full turns.

Outside Ski Turn

Steve Mahre executes the modern parallel ski turn, emphasizing the use of one ski to make the turn. "At the beginning (first figure), my body is still compressed from the completion of the previous turn. I rise to unweight and commit myself totally to steering the new turn on the outside ski (right leg). My upward extending motion releases pressure of the skis on the snow and permits me to begin the turn. Note how the straightening of my uphill leg and hip raises the downhill ski off the snow—another signal that I've completely transferred weight to the uphill, or outside, ski. In the final figure, I steer and complete the turn through pressure on the outside ski's edge."

Note the almost perfect balance, or centering, of Steve over his turning ski.

Lateral Step onto a Flat Ski

In this traverse exercise, which should be done on moderate terrain, Phil steps off the inside edge of his downhill ski and places the uphill ski flat on the snow. Note how the straightening of his uphill leg causes the downhill ski to come off the snow.

One way to describe this step, which is preparatory to a turn, would be to call it a "searching move." Riding on a flat ski, the skier can drift momentarily, searching for the correct place and time to change direction. Then he goes onto the inside (downhill) edge of the uphill ski to initiate the turn.

Inside-Outside Move

This is a traverse in which Steve steps off the inside edge of his downhill ski onto the outside (uphill) edge of his uphill ski. On a steep slope, as here, it enables him to hold his line across the hill. At any second, however, he is prepared to initiate the turn by going off the outside edge of the uphill ski, directing the ski downhill, and steering with the inside edge of the uphill (turning) ski.

"Inside" and "outside" refer here to the edges of the skis. The inside edge is the side of the ski on the inside of your foot, next to

the inside edge of the other ski. Outside edge refers to the edge to the outside of the skier's body, on either side, and in a traverse to the uphill or downhill side. Thus, an inside-outside move is one in which the skier goes from the inside edge of one ski to the outside edge of the other ski.

At first these terms may seem confusing, but as you become accustomed to them, it becomes easier to understand the different options available to you in traversing and initiating the turn.

Inside-Outside Move, with Scissor

Here Phil executes a stepping move off the inside edge of the downhill ski to the outside edge of the uphill ski. Instead of just stepping laterally, however, he directs the uphill ski to gain a higher line, using his momentum and the force of the stepping action to climb and hold speed.

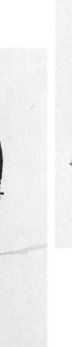

The scissoring action of the skis is seen in greater detail below. A moment later, Phil will straighten the uphill leg, bringing the downhill ski off the snow.

Note, lower right, how his body anticipates the direction of the coming turn, which he will initiate and steer by going onto the inside edge of the uphill ski.

Inside-Inside Move

In this sequence Phil steps off the inside edge of the downhill ski immediately onto the inside edge of the uphill ski. He starts in a traverse and makes a wide step onto the edge of what will be the outside, turning ski.

Quick Inside-Inside Move

From a traverse Steve steps off the inside edge of the downhill ski. Not only does he step onto the inside edge of the uphill ski, but he has already started the ski in the direction of the new turn.

In comparing this move with the ones on the previous pages, you can see how Phil and Steve are quickening the action of starting the turn. In place of the brief traverse between stepping onto the uphill ski and starting the turn (inside-outside move), the skier, using the inside-inside move, goes directly onto the edge of the turning ski. To quicken the initiation phase further, he has stepped onto the inside edge of a ski that already is pointed in the new direction.

Inside-Outside Move on Downhill Ski: White Pass Lean

Now the action of going from the traverse into the turn initiation is quickened further. Instead of starting the turn by stepping onto the uphill ski, Phil leans downhill toward the new turn, rolling onto the outside edge of his downhill ski. A split second later he will step

onto the inside edge of the outside (uphill) ski to steer the turn already started.

This is a traverse exercise to gain the feel for initiating what we call "the White Pass Turn." We also call it "the White Pass Lean" because of the way it causes the skier to lean downhill.

Inside-Outside Turn

Phil does a classic step turn, going from the inside edge of the downhill ski to the outside edge of the uphill ski, executing a brief traverse, and then initiating the turn by going onto the inside edge of the uphill ski. Today still—and for years past—this has been the classic giant slalom turn. And for good reason.

The inside-outside turn is ideally suited to long, back-and-forth turns across the hill. Here Phil traverses, with angulation, on the downhill ski coming out of the previous turn. He steps off the downhill ski with force (see the bending arc of the ski), and the energy gained from the deflexing ski aids the lateral step while giving him forward momentum. He steps onto the uphill ski, using its outside edge to hold his line across the hill. Finally he initiates the new turn by tipping onto the inside edge of the uphill ski.

Inside-Inside Move with Hop

Throughout this book we have stressed the importance of independent leg action in skiing. Here Steve exaggerates the action of an inside-inside move to demonstrate how the legs should work independently of one another.

Traversing across the hill, he springs off the inside edge of his downhill ski, lifting his skis completely off the snow. In the air, he effortlessly pivots his body in the direction of the new turn and then lands on the inside edge of the outside ski, which steers the turn. Note the easy flexing action of the outside leg as it absorbs the landing.

The inside-inside turn, with hop, also occurs when a skier comes off a roll or bump and is thrown in the air. With the skis in the air and not subject to friction of the snow, the skier can quickly initiate the turn by pivoting the body downhill. Then he lands on the inside edge of the outside ski to steer and complete the turn.

The White Pass Turn

The way this turn got started is curious, and tells a lot about what potentially can go wrong—and right—when a coach and a racer interact.

Almost from the time he first coached us, Harald Schoenhaar was bothered by what appeared to be a flaw in Steve's technique. What Harald saw was Steve getting onto the inside ski early in his turns. It looked like a basic technique error, but something else was curious about it.

Harald saw this inside-ski move in a number of World Cup races where Steve was finishing near the top, competing against the best racers in the world. As a coach and technical analyst, Harald was baffled. Here was what appeared to be a textbook technique error, but the clock at the finish line was saying that it wasn't.

We discussed the situation with Harald and began to analyze the pros and cons of what the inside ski move really meant. Soon we began to realize that it wasn't an error but rather an instinctive move developed by a racer to get more quickly from gate to gate on fast terrain.

White Pass Turn (*continued*)

As we practiced the move Harald saw more and more benefits to it. He christened it "the White Pass Turn" after the name of the ski area where we learned to race as youngsters. We added to it "the White Pass Lean," because it calls for the skier to lean downhill in a pronounced way in the initiation phase of the turn.

Here, Phil is seen executing the turn on the hill at White Pass, above the home where we grew up.

White Pass Turn, Rear View

The White Pass Turn actually is a quick and subtle move from the inside edge of the downhill ski onto its outside edge. Phil starts in a traverse and rolls onto the downhill (outside) edge of the downhill ski.

"It's a move that enables the racer to go from one turn to the next and do it a lot quicker. Instead of using a glide phase between turns, or a step and then glide, I fall over the downhill ski and lean into the next turn. As the turn progresses, I begin to angulate and then increase the angulation and pressure on the inside edge of the turning ski to complete the turn.

"I lean in to start the turn, then angulate my upper body out to complete the turn, following the outside ski. This leaves me leaning into the next turn, ready to start another White Pass Turn. I can go continuously down the hill this way."

"The White Pass Turn" is a technique to apply when there's not a lot of distance between turns. They are quick back-and-forth turns, with little time in between. They're best used in giant slalom when the change of direction and conditions allow. On the other hand, if there is distance between gates—calling for a traverse and a glide— you should step onto the uphill ski in a more or less pronounced way to start the turn.

White Pass Turn, Top View

"Most skiers will find the turn a little awkward to do initially," says Phil. "But as you go on, it feels more and more natural, especially in turns where you're carrying pretty good speed, going across the fall line and finishing each turn. It shouldn't be used on flat terrain or in making half-turns, as in slalom or short-swing skiing, because you'll fall over. You have to finish the turn.

"The White Pass Turn normally is used on a steeper hill that calls for greater angulation. You follow the downhill ski to finish the turn, then roll it over on its downhill edge to quickly initiate the new turn.

"This is a turn that the good recreational skier can definitely use in making giant slalom turns on advanced intermediate to steeper terrain that is groomed.

"It proved very effective during our racing careers in certain sections of courses."

Sum-up

We have seen that today's good skier has a choice in the way he or she prepares and initiates a turn. The skier can step onto a flat or edged ski—using the outside or inside edge—to make the turn. The choice of what turn to make depends on terrain, snow, and where the skier needs to make the turn, defined in race courses by the positioning of the gates. A choice of tactics creates a choice of what kind of turn to make. This will be discussed in Sections 5 and 6.

Finally it is important to remember that the steering and completion phases of the turn must be executed correctly. The turn is initiated on the balls of the feet, and as steering and completion take place, the skier increasingly pressures the tails of the skis with the heels.

The skier who not only starts but finishes the turn on the balls of the feet doesn't get the energy he or she is potentially able to extract from the ski. The forces of the turn store energy in the tail of the ski. In finishing one turn you should be able to use that energy to start the next turn, and the only way to do it is to finish on the heels.

FOUR

THE U.S. SKI TEAM

Ski racing is a progression. From the time we were very young there were rungs in a ladder to be climbed. We went from age eight category to nine–ten and eleven–twelve . . . novice to intermediate to expert class. We competed locally, then regionally against better and better racers. From regional competition we climbed to national racing—Junior Nationals, Senior Nationals, the Can-Am (now Nor-Am) circuit.

At each rung the competition becomes stiffer. If you think you're top dog in your own division, there comes the sudden jolt of being beaten by better skiers from other parts of the country and seasoned racers on the U.S. Ski Team.

The goal is to make the U.S. Ski Team. That's the ticket to Europe and the Olympics. From national competition you go to international competition. You climb to the highest rungs on the ladder— first, the Europa Cup, then World Cup competition. That's the top. You're among the best in your own country; now you must struggle again from poor starting positions. It's the worst jolt of all—a shock that many young racers, whether American, Canadian, Australian, Russian, or Japanese, can't handle.

Arriving in the Alps to compete against the international racing stars is not so much like reaching the top of a ladder; it's actually more like arriving at the bottom of a new ladder. You've been pushed back to when you were a kid, a rookie. You've made your national ski team, but now you have to look up again.

This was the picture for us when Phil made the U.S. Ski Team in 1973 at the age of sixteen, and Steve a year later. Phil made it first because of his excellent results in the 1973 Spring Series.

"Later that fall I went to the U.S. Ski Team training camp at Crystal Mountain in Washington. I wasn't particularly impressed by what I found. There were a lot of rebels on the team at the time, like Tyler Palmer. The racers didn't take the coaches or themselves seriously.

"It had to do with the times. A generation of kids in the late 1960s and the early 1970s experimented with drugs. There was Kent State. Racers fought with the team coaches over dress, hair length, diet. A lot of things were going on in the minds of the skiers that were unrelated to racing, and it was getting in the way of what they were really there to accomplish. It was a period when the French Ski Team went on the skids, too, right after the Killy era.

"From the moment I joined the ski team for training, I could see why it hadn't been as competitive as it should have been, and why things didn't run as smoothly as they should.

"Mickey Cochran was the coach when I arrived. He didn't experience great success, but I don't think it was his fault. He had inherited a group of rebels. The racers did whatever they wanted to do. My first experience of training camp was so bad I didn't care if I was involved or not."

Mickey Cochran was the father of the Cochran kids. Marilyn was a top racer on the World Cup, Barbara Ann won the gold medal in slalom at the 1972 Winter Olympics. Bobby Cochran was one of the best men skiers on the U.S. Team. And as if three weren't enough, the youngest Cochran, Lindy, also became a member of the team in the mid-1970s. Here was a father who had raised and personally coached four kids to make the ski team. If he could do that, it was reasoned, why not appoint him as coach of the whole ski team?

It sounded like a great idea, but what Mickey had been able to accomplish with his own youngsters back at their own ski hill in Vermont didn't carry over to the U.S. Ski Team.

The fact is that a coach can do only so much. Most of it is up to the athlete. Mickey had four kids of his own who were determined

These first U.S. Ski Team uniforms felt good after wearing hand-me-downs for years. Though making the team was tops in America, the real summit was a long way off.

Another skiing family was the Cochrans of Vermont: (left to right, front) Bob, Barbara Ann, Marilyn, and Lindy, with their parents behind them. Father Mickey coached the U.S. Ski Team when Phil first joined.

to go places. On the other hand, by the time he got to be national head coach, he had a U.S. Ski Team made up of racers who by no means had the motivation or desire of his own children.

Even Mickey's kids had to do it for themselves; he couldn't do it for them.

As time went by, the rebels left the ski team and a new generation arrived. We were there and became part of it. We had escaped drugs, thanks to our family background and because we lived at the ski area away from town and the availability of drugs. We knew plenty of kids who were users. They respected us for not using drugs. We never even experimented with them.

If we had been raised in a town environment it's possible we might have become involved with drugs. Athletes fool themselves. Even immersion in athletics is no guarantee a person will stay off drugs. Look at the professional football and basketball athletes for whom cocaine is a status drug.

But in ski racing there is nothing that is helped by drugs—or steroids or pep pills. It's a sport of quickness, concentration, and precision.

Not only was our arrival on the U.S. Ski Team separate, we wouldn't go to Europe together until the winter of 1975–76.

After Phil made the team following the 1973 training camp, he returned to White Pass and broke his leg in the avalanche. That winter of 1973–74, while Phil was at home and at school, scratching away with coat hangers shoved inside his cast, Steve competed on the Canadian-American Trophy series. At the age of sixteen, he led all the other racers in points for much of the season.

"After not making the team the season before, I knew how critical these races were to my being selected. The 1976 Winter Olympics were only two years away.

"Because of my success on the Can-Am circuit, and then the Spring Series, I was named to the team in 1974. I was looking forward to going to Europe with Phil."

It was not to happen. Phil had been impatient to recover from his leg fracture. "I became active too quickly. As soon as I got out of the cast, I began to run around. I went to a training camp at Mount Hood, but I felt discomfort in my boot whenever I skied. I don't think the leg ever properly healed.

"In the summer I went water skiing. We were camped by the Columbia River, near a playground. I started horsing around on a slide. I picked up speed and hit the bottom hard with my feet, and instantly felt the leg break again in the same place. Back in Yakima the doctors had to perform a sliding bone graft, inserting four screws in my leg. I was crushed. I would miss my senior year of football, which was actually more of a letdown than not skiing."

While Phil performed rehab on his leg, Steve went with the U.S. Ski Team B contingent to Europe, racing on the World Cup for the first time. "It was quite a change. For one thing, I got a uniform and all the travel was arranged. I didn't have to worry about expense at every step of the way. I could get all the coaching I wanted. But I was also at the bottom of the ladder again. I had late starting numbers and had to ski in the ruts. I placed high in a number of first runs in slalom, but then I fell in the second runs. I was no longer among the best, as I'd been when I competed in the States. I was a small fish in a big pond.

"Inconsistency is the enemy of the American men skiers who've tried to race well in Europe over the years, and I was no exception in my first winter on the World Cup. I made too many mistakes. I failed to put many back-to-back runs together. Like some past American racers in Europe—notably the Palmer brothers—I was skiing as fast as the world's top skiers, but I didn't have the consistency to make it to the finish line in a great many races.

"I was surprised at the attitude of many of the U.S. racers. There seemed to be an attitude of not wanting to race too much, as if guys were afraid of getting worn out in the starting gate. They didn't want to practice very hard either. I liked to train in the gates five or six hours a day, while most of the kids were satisfied with a couple of hours.

"The coaches were willing to train the kids as long as they wanted, but it appeared the kids didn't have a lot of desire to do so.

"Training in the gates is a must. The more time you spend on skis, the better your timing and the better your feel for your skis and the snow. The U.S. Team should have been struggling to succeed, but they weren't putting in the training hours."

After an undistinguished season the ski team returned to the United States for the National Championships in February. And now Phil reappeared on the scene, looking somewhat peaked—thin, underweight, pale, and apparently out of condition—but back on skis after a year and a half of forced idleness.

The National Championships were held at Mission Ridge, Washington, a hill we knew well from past Spring Series. On hand were the best American racers, fresh from the World Cup in Europe.

In the giant slalom Phil had bib number 22. He slashed and carved down the relatively flat course and, in a remarkable comeback, won the race. Everybody was astounded, including the coaches. Phil had been out of competition for eighteen months, yet he was able to beat all the top racers on the U.S. Ski Team.

Earning a Good Starting Position (Steve)

The start, or bib, number worn by a ski racer is important and usually critical to the outcome of a race. The lower a racer's start number, the better the snow conditions on the course, and the easier it is to ski. As more and more racers come down the course, it becomes rutted and harder to ski.

Racers earn early starting positions by improving their results. The better your results, the higher the seeding group you can move into.

Seeding groups are established by the FIS (Federation Internationale de Ski). In FIS-sanctioned races all over the world, racers earn points. By earning good (low) FIS points a racer graduates to a higher seeded group.

The best racers in the world are in the first group of fifteen each—in slalom, giant slalom, and downhill. They get the right to start from first to fifteenth in the first run of a World Cup or Olympic race. The second-seeded group starts sixteenth to thirtieth. They have pretty good snow conditions, too, to race on. After that the courses deteriorate and it's harder to get good results.

Downhill, of course, is a one-run event. In slalom and giant slalom the starting order of the racers in the second run is determined by the results of the first run. The top five start in reverse order of their finish, so that, for example, the fastest racer from the first run starts fifth in the second run. After that all the racers in the second run start in the order of their first-run finishes.

In 1974, when I first arrived in Europe, I found myself in the third and fourth seeding groups, sometimes starting with a bib number in the sixties. Even with a late starting number, I occasionally was able to get results in the first fifteen—in one run, at least. But it wasn't easy.

Ski racing is kind of a catch-22. You need better starting positions to get results, but it's hard to get good results without a better starting position. It took two more winters before I could start in the first seed.

"It was as if I'd never been away, though I certainly felt it because physically I was still in poor shape, and I hated the feel of the screws in my leg.

"Mentally, though, it was a breakthrough—a key one in my career. I went on to compete on the tail end of the World Cup circuit and placed twelfth in a race at Garibaldi in British Columbia. It was an eye-opener for me and everyone else, my being able to do this after not skiing for so long. When the season ended in April, I went immediately to the hospital and had the screws removed.

"It had been a short winter of competition, but in those few, brief results I'd established my right to go with the ski team to Europe the next season for the Winter Olympics at Innsbruck."

Steve, too, showed what he could do at the National Championships, winning the slalom. The press was calling us the two best ski racers in the United States. We appeared in *Sports Illustrated.*

In the late summer of 1975 the U.S. Ski Team, as it often does, held a training camp at Portillo, Chile, in the Andes. For a couple of eighteen-year-olds, it was an exciting trip. After landing in Santiago we rode by train up into the mountains, the snow growing deeper as we ascended into the winter of the southern hemisphere.

Portillo is a remote place, difficult to get in and out of. The plan was to be there for three weeks. When we arrived none of our gear could be found. For the first week we skied in old Caber boots, blue jeans, and coats. Finally the situation got to Steve: "We were wearing the same clothes for skiing, eating, and sitting around. There was nowhere to go. The training wasn't very useful because we didn't have our own gear. I missed my girlfriend, Debbie. I told the coach, Hank Tauber, I was going home. 'What are we going to do with this guy?' Tauber asked. 'He has so much talent, but skiing means so little to him that he'd rather go home.' But I was homesick, and I left.

"Phil stayed. He had a more determined, aggressive attitude, which would show up the following ski season in Europe when he moved ahead of me. He tolerated the travel better and was more capable than I of meeting people and making friends. He enjoyed himself, while my routine was to have dinner and go back to the room and be bored."

Phil experienced an incident at Portillo that led to a scene with Cindy Nelson, who has skied longer for the U.S. Ski Team than any racer in its history.

"Cindy's a fierce competitor whom I admire. She's sometimes called 'the Queen of the Ski Team' because she has led the girls for so many years. She had come to train at Portillo too. There isn't much to do there at night. All the athletes—including racers from other countries—hang around the hotel, hemmed in by these huge mountains. We were all living in a building called the Octagon.

"One weekend the coaches decided to give us a night off, but they warned us to be in the sack by eleven and not repeat the rowdy behavior of the French Ski Team the night before.

"I was with Billy Taylor, another U.S. racer and a good friend. We were young and out on a big trip for the first time. The dancing in the hotel didn't start until eleven, and most of the team decided to keep out of trouble with the bosses and quickly left for bed. Billy and I stayed on.

Cindy Nelson, a fierce competitor, fought with Phil over some nighttime high-jinks in Portillo. Later, they made up.   SUSAN HUFF

"The party got better and better. I lost a contact lens dancing, and the crowd must have danced on it for a couple of hours. Somehow I managed to find it the next day. At 1:30 A.M., Billy and I called it quits.

"We'd had more to drink than we should have. We stumbled back through the snow to the Octagon, then sat on the steps outside talking. For some reason we decided that we didn't favor Lindy Cochran spending time with Ken Read, the Canadian downhiller. We climbed the stairs inside the Octagon, making known in loud voices our opinions of Lindy's taste in men. Since we didn't know what room Lindy was in, we stopped at every door to advertise ourselves.

"When we reached the top of the stairs Cindy Nelson burst out of her room and began screaming at us, 'There are serious skiers at Portillo, and you should have the decency to be quiet.'

"I replied that we were having fun, she was having fun, and everything was cool. I guess I said more too. At breakfast the next morning we came in late. Dave Currier, the downhiller, cried out, 'Hey, Nightmare!' I looked around and he said, 'Yeah, you. I couldn't go back to sleep last night, it was so funny.' But Cindy didn't think it was funny. She hardly would talk to me for the next five years. At the New York Ski Ball in 1980 we were reminiscing about old times and that night in Portillo was brought up. By now we were both able to laugh about it and became good friends."

We wondered sometimes why Cindy didn't hang up her skis and retire. She had been with the ski team since 1971 and had been on four Olympic teams. She won a bronze medal in the downhill in 1976 and a silver medal at the World Ski Championships in 1982. We thought she might retire then, but she loved racing too much.

We never liked summer ski-race training, either in the United States or Europe. We even feel it taught us bad habits. The snow is unnatural and often treated with chemicals. It isn't like skiing on natural snow. When we trained in summer we found ourselves having to work in fall training to rid ourselves of the effects of the summer, to recapture the old feel for our skis that we had lost while training. The best season we ever enjoyed competitively—1982— followed a summer of no training. By that time we could call our own shots, and we told the coaches we wanted no part of summer skiing.

There's a fine line in determining what a racer should decide for himself, and what authority the coaches should wield. It has to be a trade-off. Coaches learn from athletes, and athletes learn from coaches.

If a coach says to a competitor, "We want you to do things this way," and the kid doesn't succeed, then there's something wrong with the system, or the way the coaches are applying it.

Racers must have enough strength and belief in themselves so that if they pursue their goals in a self-determined way, they'll be successful. A program that attempts to rub out that initiative won't work. That has happened to the U.S. Ski Team periodically as well as to European teams.

The coach must be aware of what the individual competitor needs and what he doesn't need, what he should be doing and what he shouldn't. If a kid says, "I don't want to ski all summer," and the coach believes he should ski, then the two should sit down together and talk it out. They need to compromise. The coach might say, "You do need to ski this summer, but let's focus on a time period and what I think you need to accomplish specifically in your training."

Differences between athletes and coaches have been illustrated, and still are, by the adjustments European coaches make when they come to work for the U.S. Ski Team. Harald Schoenhaar, who helped us put together the instruction in this book, arrived in the States when we first came on board in 1974. He hardly spoke English. Harald had been the coach of the German National Ski Team and is a graduate of one of the renowned *Sportsschule* there.

Coming to coach American kids was an eye-opener for Harald. Originally he had very set ways about how he was going to run his program. In Europe he was accustomed to tighter discipline. He saw us American kids as lax. Then he learned that his ways were not our ways. The admirable thing about Harald is that he is flexible. He was prepared to change his thinking. He had his points, and we had ours, and we arrived at a good blend.

Schoenhaar was able to improve himself as a coach because he

Our coach, Harald Schoenhaar, at first found American kids lax. But he was a good listener, and the blend finally worked.   *PURO CONSTANTINO*

listened to athletes. He learned our mentality. The sport of skiing is different in the United States, just as we go about our lives differently here.

In Europe a coach like Charlie Kahr of the Austrian Ski Team is virtually a national hero. The whole country is rooting for the team at a level of interest such as we see only in, say, the National Football League. Charlie Kahr is like an Austrian Tom Landry or Don Shula.

European coaches come from a setting where skiing is a sport of national importance. They can, and do, rule the members of their teams (perhaps not the stars) with an iron hand.

As with football players here, Austrian ski racers know that skiing is a way to fame and fortune, so they go along with a demanding coach—usually. But if a European coach tries to exert the same authority here, he finds opposition.

European coaches who have come to the United States have difficulty understanding the mentality of the American kids—kids who view ski racing as maybe not the most important thing in their lives. Then, gradually, the Europeans come around in their views. There's been give and take.

At one time the directors of the U.S. Ski Team were opposed to employing European coaches. The prevailing view was that we had to have American coaches for American kids because only American coaches could understand American skiers.

The idea that America could go it alone in ski racing, without help from abroad, was plain wrongheaded. To be competitive in the World Cup, we had to have European trainers and coaches. The American coaches simply lacked the experience.

Eighty percent of all the races are held in Europe. It's essential to hire coaches familiar with the scene there, who've picked up knowledge from the other teams, who can go into jury meetings and even argue the American point of view in German or French.

An American coach who goes to Europe for the first time is hardly better able to cope with the unfamiliar situation than a racer. He's as much in awe of what he sees as the kids under his charge. With an experienced European coach who has been on the World Cup circuit that isn't the case.

We think the U.S. Team is now in good shape with coaches. In 1985 the Alpine program director was German, the men's technical coach French, and the downhill coach Swiss.

The progress of U.S. Ski Team coaching has been remarkable. The winter after we retired, the team hired J. P. Chatelard, a Frenchman, as men's coach in slalom and giant slalom. Chatelard had worked with the Swedish National Ski Team. There wasn't much he could do with Ingemar Stenmark—already the best technical skier in the world—so he concentrated on a bunch of young Swedish racers. Occasionally one of them beat Stenmark, which amused Chatelard no end. By the same token, Theo Nadig, the U.S. downhill coach, once worked with the 1984 World Cup champion, Pirmin Zurbriggen.

We mentioned before how at the time we arrived on the Ski Team scene, ten years earlier, some of the rebellious racers were leaving. By 1975 they had been replaced by guys like Geoff Bruce, Greg Jones, Cary Adgate, and Pete Patterson. The new guys were inconsistent, but occasionally one of them would do something.

Schoenhaar arrived in 1974, hired by Hank Tauber, who'd just become the Alpine program director. Tauber is an American from Gloversville, New York, but he is of Swiss parentage. He speaks German, even in the Swiss dialect, *Schwyzerdüetsch.* He's as much at home in Europe as he is in the States, where he also once coached the girls' team. With the arrival of Tauber as Alpine director, the effort of the team completed its turn from negative to positive.

As leader of the ski team, Tauber demanded the best. If he put his own time into something, he expected to get results. Some of the racers resented him, but we liked him, and we believe he helped the team a lot.

Alpine Director Hank Tauber took a personal interest in our careers and was instrumental in setting up our first contracts. K2 PHOTO

From the beginning Hank understood our own family situation, that our parents didn't have the financial means to help us, and he had a grasp of the changes that were coming about in international skiing in the mid-1970s. The FIS had taken the lead to liberalize payments to competitors within the Olympics system. It became possible for manufacturers to pay money to racers through their national ski associations. We could start to make a living at what we were doing. And racers who previously had to quit and find jobs could stay in racing, gaining more experience and skill.

A racer now had the opportunity to reach his true potential. Previously he had to think about going to college or finding a job because there wasn't enough money to stick with the Ski Team.

The whole financial situation changed. Hank Tauber understood the technicalities. He was in touch with the international authorities and as a result was able—and willing—to represent us with ski equipment manufacturers and make certain we got a square deal.

Hank was not a strong ski coach as such. You could tell that from watching him ski. The same was true of Bill Marolt, who succeeded Hank as Alpine program director. When we watched Marolt ski we couldn't imagine him coaching us. But the difference between Tauber and Marolt was that Tauber stayed away from the Ski Team on the hill and generally avoided making comments about the technique of the racers. Marolt, on the other hand, might be inclined to say, "You know, I was on the hill the other day, and I saw that you weren't planting your pole. I'll come out tomorrow and we'll set some gates, and we'll work on that pole plant."

Steve would think to himself, Hey, Bill, I've been training with the coaches for three months. You come in and in one hour decide that the only reason I'm not having results is because I'm not planting my pole?

In that particular instance the problem was actually more with Steve's boots. We got the plastic changed, and his skiing came back.

Any Alpine program director has to stay out of the way of the hill coaches. For Harald Schoenhaar that was difficult. Nevertheless, after succeeding Marolt, he had the good sense to hire one of the best hill coaches in the world, J. P. Chatelard.

Schoenhaar is a superior coach. We used to see him try things on skis that we'd never seen before, and in fact Harald is a better glider than we are. He could probably teach us new things.

It's a great temptation for anyone who has coached to interfere. The classic case is when someone who coached you when you were younger catches up with you one day years later when you're on the National Ski Team. You may have just come back from Europe to the National Championships. The Ski Team coaches have been working on you for several months to correct a flaw in your skiing. Now the old coach from your division is on the scene and he's saying to you "Try this, try that" while you listen politely. But the Ski Team coach is horrified. He hears it and says to himself, "I've been trying to get the kid not to ski that way all winter, and now a stranger appears trying to get him to do it again."

It's all too easy for coaches to mix kids up. One of the great improvements introduced by Harald Schoenhaar has been to make the coaching system more uniform. Just before he took over his present job as Alpine program director, Schoenhaar headed the U.S. Ski Coaches Association. As a result of his work the team no longer has to deal so much with kids coming out of one program only to find themselves having to do things completely differently at the National Ski Team level. He persuaded the regional coaches to adopt the same drills used by the Ski Team, such as the long turn-short turn drills shown in this book. Coaches are now certified. And with uniform drills there is less inclination at the National Ski Team level to change a kid's style of skiing. Now everyone is focusing on the fundamentals of technique, and kids can slide more easily from one program to another.

We've been asked if we'd like to coach. Even though there's a wealth of technique we can pass on to skiers, we're not certain we'd make good coaches. Skiing and proficiency in ski racing came easily to us. It's quite possible that someone who has never been a great skier himself could be a better coach.

Mickey Cochran was never a champion skier but he coached his four children onto the U.S. Ski Team. He had to work for it and think a lot about ski racing but he certainly got the results. Did he push them or did his kids just like racing, the way we did?

Paralleling the fact that American racers have always been at somewhat of a disadvantage in competing so much abroad, it's significant that when European racers come to the United States to compete they usually don't ski to their potential. They have to overcome the culture shock of language, different food and restaurant service, strange transportation and hotels. They don't have their own team cars to whiz around in, as they have in Europe, where they may be able to drive home for a couple of days between races. They have to ride a bus and they have to figure out how to get to the race site.

Suddenly they encounter an alien environment, just as the U.S. Ski Team does when it goes to Europe. The difference is that we have to race 70 to 80 percent of the time over there, while they have to race only 20 percent of their time in North America.

Still, that's the name of the game. To win the World Cup you have to be able to compete in all countries. In 1984—85, for example, the men's and women's World Cup went to nine countries, including Japan.

The travel is difficult, but it's our opinion that past American thinking has been overly anxious about introducing young racers to Europe too early in their careers. If a kid is winning at the national level the only way he or she can become excellent is by going to Europe.

It's true we've had kids who have competed well nationally in the States and have fallen apart when they crossed the Atlantic. They seem to disintegrate; they can't ski. Then they come home and within a couple of weekends they're winning again, even occasionally beating Europeans they lost races to in the Alps.

Ski racing for Americans in Europe is a test of mental toughness. Christin Cooper, the American silver medalist in giant slalom at the 1984 Winter Olympics, serves as a marvelous example of what it takes to win. When we first saw her ski in Europe we were unimpressed. But Christin was a fierce competitor. She knew what was needed to win and she executed.

One factor that helped Christin when she competed outside the States was that she was outgoing. She liked to have fun. There was an occasion at Furano, in Japan, when she approached Ingemar

Stenmark and asked him to dance. Everyone knows that Ingemar is painfully shy. But Christin wasn't going to take no for an answer. She grabbed Ingemar by the arm and dragged him out on the dance floor. It didn't appear he liked to dance, and Christin was probably the only one who could make him do it.

Christin was friendly. She never thought of herself as special, and she never insisted that people look up to her. It was this attitude that helped her succeed when she raced in Europe.

The racers who make it in the World Cup are the ones who can put aside the differences in culture, language, food, even the absence of simple things like a john in the room. They must be able to separate these things from their ski racing. They must be able to affirm to themselves "The only reason I'm here is ski racing."

You hear U.S. racers complain about the travel and being away

Outgoing Christin Cooper showed how to adjust in competing abroad. She even got shy Swedish superstar Ingemar Stenmark on the dance floor.

from home. But we were homesick too. What made us different from many racers who'd come before us was that we were determined to focus on ski racing. In that sense we psyched ourselves to believe that what we were doing in Europe wasn't really different from competing at home. Granted, the crowds were bigger and the events were more elaborately organized, but the courses, the rules of the sport, the equipment, and the technique were the same.

Many American racers become depressed by the fact that they can't climb the ladder to the top in Europe as fast as they progressed at home. Steve was affected: "It took me three years internationally to advance myself as much as I had in the U.S. in three months. When I was thirteen years old, for example, I moved from the lowest class in my division to the highest class in a season. When I was fifteen I was beating eighteen- and twenty-year-olds in my division.

"On the World Cup it took me four years before I could win a race. I even quit at one point. Only mental toughness carried me through the experience. I had to generate the will to keep going. Of course I had an advantage—I had a brother with me. Wherever I went, he went. Still, it wasn't easy."

Our close relationship as brothers and friends was undoubtedly an asset the other U.S. racers didn't have. Without close friends on the team they had to learn to live with other racers as well as adjust to different coaches. They had to learn to adapt to more variables, including being in Europe itself.

Ski racing is an individual sport, but it's also a team sport. It's practically impossible for a racer to go on his own to Europe to compete, without the Ski Team.

Training times have to be scheduled. You have to live within an organization, a structure, and in our society not all kids are willing to conform to structure. Those who couldn't take the ski team structure sometimes took parting shots at the system. They'd say, "The ski team program just wasn't made for me."

Well, the program wasn't made for Phil and Steve Mahre, either. But we went along with it.

It's true that after 1980 we didn't go along entirely with the team's training program. We refused to ski in the summer. But the team officials knew that if they had insisted on our training in summer, we would have retired from the ski team.

Good coaches will know when to be lenient and when it's right for a racer to take time off. If the kid comes back skiing better, the next time the coach will listen. But if the kid doesn't come back skiing better, the chances are it was a cop-out. He has some other problem that's bothering him.

Strange as it seems, peer pressure on the younger racers can be such that to excel—to gain a berth on the A team—can actually be frowned upon. This problem surfaced in 1981 when the Ski Team was about to go to Scandinavia for a series of World Cup races. Many of the younger team members were not having success. Alpine Director Bill Marolt took us to tea one afternoon to ask our opinion of what could be done.

"Interview each of them individually, Bill," we suggested. "Ask each guy what he wants to do.

"Make them be honest with themselves, as well as with you. They've been in Europe a month with no decent results. They've been beaten badly. It's their first time here. We think most of them really want to go home, but if they say only what they think the coaches want to hear, they'll claim they want to go to Scandinavia."

Instead of talking to the racers individually, though, Bill took it on himself to send them all home, with one exception—our friend Johnny Buxman, who had been showing some promise.

Johnny awoke the next morning to say good-bye to his teammates. They wouldn't talk to him. They seemed to resent the fact they were in the minor leagues while Johnny had been promoted to the majors.

"Am I supposed to feel bad for doing well?" Johnny asked us.

Buxman was being put down by his teammates for wanting to succeed.

The pressure to be a good guy, to go along with the attitude of teammates, doesn't develop a winning mentality. In 1981 it plagued the ski team.

Friend and teammate John Buxman
was plagued by inconsistency.
When he did get promoted on
the team the other racers resented it.

SKI MAGAZINE

A racer can't race for his buddies. We don't race for the team, our mother, father, coaches, or even each other. As close as we are, each of us races for himself, to realize his own success.

One solution that has been suggested to make life easier for U.S. racers in Europe is to create a central, European home away from home. Frankly, we don't see how that could work. For one thing, you'd never find a single location in Europe that the racers could reach conveniently. If the so-called Ski Team Home were near Zurich, Switzerland, and you were at a race in Val d'Isère, what sense would it make to go there between races if the next competition was at Sestriere, in Italy? It's a lot easier to drive to Sestriere and get settled in a new hotel.

The solution to all these problems is to have racers with the mental toughness to handle heavy travel and being away from home for long periods. Trying to become one of the best ski racers in the world should in itself be worth all the hassle. Ingemar Stenmark, who is from a small town north of the Arctic Circle, hardly ever competed at home. He was constantly on the road, and he won more World Cup races than any skier in history. If you want to be the best, you have to make sacrifices.

To most observers the U.S. Ski Team seems to have progressed considerably in the last ten years. Fund-raising obviously is much better. The budget has gone from a million dollars to over four million. Unfortunately, this has also created a bureaucracy.

When we first joined the World Cup we had the impression that the team had more active people on the hill than in the back office. Now the reverse seems to be true. Like the Army, we should try to get as many of our troops on the front lines as we can.

In our early years the organization was good. Every day we had video cameras available in training. The fund-raising may not have been as strong as it is now, but what's the use of having funds if they aren't being put to the best use? In our later years we felt that the communication between coaches, athletes, and office deteriorated. It didn't affect us because we were working off the input of the previous six years, but it might have hurt the other kids. The team also had become too media oriented.

Obviously the Ski Team has to be publicized and promoted, but many times we found this overdone. Some of the racers resented it. Bill Koch talked to us about it and his views are interesting, though we don't necessarily agree with them.

Bill is a quiet, gifted guy who calls his own shots. People remember him for winning the silver medal in the thirty-kilometer cross-country race at the Innsbruck Olympics, but we think his 1982 World Cup championship was more significant, just as we think that winning the season-long Alpine World Cup—including slalom,

Bill Koch didn't see eye to eye with us on dealing with the Ski Team. A quiet, gifted guy, Kochie calls his own shots.

g.s., and downhill events—is a greater achievement than an Olympic gold medal in a single race.

As a cross-country skier, Kochie found more problems with the Ski Team than we did on the Alpine side. Even while Nordic skiers lacked the sponsorships that brought us money, Bill saw the team making unreasonable promotional demands—an issue that would arise later with Bill Johnson, the downhiller.

Kochie began to talk to us about fund-raisers and publicity functions. He asked us how we handled the requests. We said we were fairly easygoing and often made appearances for the team to raise money. Bill, on the other hand, mostly refused to make appearances. He thought his job was to race, and to leave the fund-raising to others.

Bill believed in making things better for the athletes on the team, but much of what he talked about seemed to revolve around the welfare of the top racers. He thought that if a team sponsor wanted to promote their product using Bill Koch, then he should get more reward for it. More recently Bill Johnson has been saying essentially the same thing.

We sympathize with some of their ideas but don't see eye to eye on others. When Johnson says he should get 80 percent of the sponsor money, and the team the other 20 percent, we say, "Fine, do it. But then pay for your own travel and coaching and all the other things the team pays for and organizes. Moreover, if you take most of the money, what's going to pay for the training of young racers? How's anybody going to succeed you?"

Increasingly the U.S. Ski Team will face problems in dealing with superstars and money—problems they didn't face with us.

FIVE

LEARNING HOW TO WIN

From the beginning of our international racing careers we competed against Ingemar Stenmark, a totally dedicated master technician of skiing who is a year older than we. It was like trying to be home-run king in the era of Babe Ruth.

In every run, no matter how well we skied, there was always the specter of Ingemar. If he was ahead after one run, we had to try to catch him. Or, if he was a few split seconds behind, he was ready to pounce on you.

Ingemar was a prodigy. In his eighteenth year he already placed twelfth in the overall World Cup. He was nineteen when he won both the slalom and giant slalom titles, twenty when he won the first of three consecutive World Cups. By comparison Phil didn't win his first World Cup until he was twenty-four.

Ski racing was all that mattered to Ingemar. He came from the small town of Tarnaby, 500 miles north of Stockholm, close to "the land of the midnight sun," an area with few daylight hours in winter.

As a teenager he kept a photograph of the World Cup pinned on the wall of his room. The Swedish racer Stig Strand, also from Tarnaby, once told us that Ingemar became so obsessed with winning the World Cup and trained so hard that Stig virtually never saw him, not easy in a town of seven hundred people.

We trained extensively with Ingemar in the mid-1970s, often practicing on the same courses. With Ingemar it was not the amount of training or number of runs he practiced that was important, but rather the intensity he put into his training. You could see it when he skied, the total concentration. He knew better than any other racer how to separate what was happening on the hill and what was happening off the hill. He had the ability to keep extraneous thoughts out of his mind and to focus strictly on racing.

Phil with Ingemar Stenmark at the finish line. It was like trying to be home-run king in the era of Babe Ruth.   TEAM RUSSELL

Even though we rated him the best technical (slalom and giant slalom) skier in the world, we knew there were days he was beatable. "One day," Phil says, "if I kept working at it, I knew I could be better than he was. But it took a frustratingly long time.

"I'd won over him occasionally before, but my most memorable victory came at Åre in Sweden in 1981. There Ingemar had the home crowd cheering for him. It was a World Cup slalom race, and after the first run he was just 3/100ths of a second ahead of me. We were both about seven tenths of a second behind the leaders.

"In the second run Ingemar was in the starting gate, running just before me. If he won the race he would set a new record for the number of World Cup competitions won by a single competitor. He had a blistering run that put him in the lead. The partisan Swedish crowd cheered wildly.

"As I stood waiting my turn in the starting gate, the Swedish starter shook the Swedish coach's hand and congratulated him on Stenmark's victory. The crowd meanwhile was going bananas.

"Well, that really ticked me off. I'm reminded now of Yogi Berra's famous remark, 'It isn't over until it's over.' That's how I felt. I was mad. 'This is one he isn't going to win,' I said to myself, and I uncorked one of the most aggressive slalom runs of my career. I wound up beating Stenmark's second-run time by 4/100ths of a second, and won the race by 1/100th of a second."

Ingemar's tenacity and mental stamina were greater than those of any other racer of our era. It wasn't his technique—he just wanted to win more than anyone else.

The truth is that at the top of the World Cup circuit the skiing is technically pretty much the same. The uninitiated observer may not see that, because the racers' individual styles look different. But basically they're all making the same moves. Some do it better than others—that is, with fewer mistakes. That was Ingemar. He made fewer mistakes than anyone else. He capitalized on everyone *else's* errors. His edge was not a matter of special technique—it was mental attitude.

Ingemar is modest. He doesn't boast about his victories. He'd never say, Ali-like, something like "I'm the greatest." If you wanted

Stenmark in the gates. Among the top racers, technique differences are unimportant. What Ingemar did was to capitalize on everyone else's errors.

to know what kind of a person he was, you had to look for it on the ski hill, not at a press conference.

What Ingemar did on the hill was all that mattered to him. It was as if he was saying, "Here you see me skiing. This is who I am. It's the best." He was a perfectionist. He was out to be the best he could be.

In any sport, attention to detail usually marks the difference between the champion and the second-best. Stenmark had a superior understanding of what he had to do to win, down to the last nuance. It's hard to recall a single glitch in his preparation for a race, including the final details of buckling his boots. And if something did go wrong, he believed there had to be a reason for it. In his mind there was no such thing as bad luck. If something went wrong, he was at fault, not someone else. Nothing slipped by him.

In all the years we competed we carried a mutual respect for each other. It was not a competitive, beat-the-other-guy-into-the-ground thing. He respected us if we won, and we respected him.

Our arrival on the World Cup scene coincided with a changing of champions. Gustavo Thoeni, a German-speaking Italian from the South Tirol region of northern Italy, had dominated ski racing since 1970. He won the World Cup four times, more than any man before or since.

We admired the way Thoeni skied. He was very straight up on his skis, never fell backward, yet had great knee drive. His greatest skiing probably occurred at the World Ski Championships at St. Moritz in 1974 when he won the gold medals in both slalom and giant slalom. We didn't see it, but his slalom run that day is still cited as one of the most beautiful in all of skiing.

It's hard to fathom how Thoeni skied. If we wore boots as straight up as his, and pressured the tails of the skis as he did, we would have been dragging our butts in the ground.

We admired the way Italy's Gustavo Thoeni skied. If we wore boots as straight up as his, and pressured the tails of the skis as much as he did, we would have dragged our butts on the ground.   SUN VALLEY NEWS BUREAU

He had a wonderful feel for the snow. We always admired the way he looked ahead. We used to study pictures of him coming out of a turn, approaching the next turn and already looking at what he had to do in the turn *after that.*

Just as the French and Austrians dominated world racing in the years before, the Italian ski team was a force in the early 1970s. Thoeni won his World Cups in 1971, '72, '73, and '75, while his teammate, Piero Gros, edged him out in 1974. It was the first and last time for Gros, and after 1974 his only notable victory was a gold medal in slalom at the Innsbruck Olympics.

Gros was the premier choker. There was the time we were at Fulpmes, Austria, when he was leading after the first run of a giant slalom. Strangely, he hardly inspected the course for the second run. When he ran it he missed an offset gate which he evidently didn't see and certainly hadn't remembered was there. He didn't finish the race. It happened often with Gros—he would lose his concentration.

Thoeni's era started to decline in 1975, after he won the last of his four World Cups. That was the winter he and Ingemar Stenmark were virtually tied in the World Cup at the end of the season. For the only time in the history of the World Cup the organizers had to use the ceremonial parallel race at the last meet to decide the outcome.

Thoeni won the parallel, but only after the Italian racers, representing the strongest ski team in the world at the time, conveniently managed not to win against him.

Ingemar won the World Cup the next year, and Gustavo retired three or four years later. In some ways he was the greater champion. While Stenmark refused to compete in downhill, Thoeni was a respectable downhiller. It enabled him to win the FIS combined gold medal at the 1976 Olympic Winter Games.

Stenmark and Thoeni—like the 1984 World Cup champion, Pirmin Zurbriggen of Switzerland—were intensely quiet, shy people. Ingemar is very withdrawn. We would like to have known him better, but it was hard to do so because he was difficult to talk with.

"What do you plan to do this summer?" we'd ask Ingemar.

"I go to Sweden," he answered.

Attempting to keep the conversation rolling, we'd continue, "Are you going to do some fishing?"

"Yes."

End of conversation.

Ingemar knew English, but he's such a perfectionist about everything that it may have bothered him not to speak it absolutely correctly.

He approached the sport even more intensely than we did. He was driven. Like John McEnroe on the tennis court, he seems comfortable only when he's on the ski hill. He was in his element in the finish area of a race.

Many of the great ski racers have been shy, introspective types. Even Jean-Claude Killy, the 1968 Olympic triple medal winner, was intensely shy when he was a top competitor. It may be that there is a correlation between shyness—being withdrawn—and winning ski races.

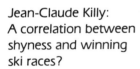

Jean-Claude Killy:
A correlation between shyness and winning ski races?

To be a champion you have to be selfish to a great degree. You have no time for other interests or people. Athletes who excel in competition have a tendency to keep things to themselves, to work things out on their own. They're reluctant to go to another person for advice. For them, solving problems on their own is like another step up the ladder.

The guy who's withdrawn—call it self-centered, if you want—actually creates time to think more about what he's doing. He has a driven, inner picture of what he has to do to be the best. Without social distractions he can zero in on what he has to accomplish and consequently will excel quicker than someone who is outer-directed. A dedicated champion is either on the ski hill or he's thinking about skiing. He has little time for anything else.

Phil was that way: "I became very self-centered. I was dedicating all of my time to becoming the best at ski racing. In that situation you don't spend enough time stimulating other growth patterns in your life—like being around people, talking with them, relating to them. Those areas of your life are put on hold.

"I kept things bottled up and wasn't open with a lot of my thoughts. Occasionally my wife would say, 'What's wrong?' and I'd reply 'Nothing,' even when something was eating me up inside. Instead I'd be thinking to myself, 'I'll deal with this. Don't worry about it.'

"I realized a difference in myself when I retired. People began to remark on how I'd become more relaxed. The weight was off my shoulders, although the pressure to perform is still there because I have to keep a professional image alive.

"Sometimes I just wish I could slow down and let life come at me more, instead of going after it. It would be nice to be a bit less aggressive. In a sense, like my father, I wanted to do the best I could. I'm aggressive in wanting to see that what I do turns out as nearly perfect as I can make it. That can drive other people batty."

The very top racers become protective about themselves as a shield against people. With the arrival of celebrity comes the difficulty of sorting out who is a friend. You have to figure out who's trying to use you, who's a phony, and who's genuine.

The matter of the top international ski stars being shy and not outgoing has drawn a lot of criticism from the press. They complain that the World Cup tour is dull because the racers are dull. They want lively personalities, more Bill Johnsons. But we don't think the press is going to find them.

The great book of historical ski results shows that few of the superstars were outstanding, outgoing personalities when they raced. Stellar personalities don't usually break through the finish line with consistently stellar times. Maybe, in skiing, too, nice guys finish last.

The American racer Greg Jones, in his final seasons on the World Cup, was an outgoing character, but it happened during the downside of his career. Today there are some lively characters on the circuit, but not many of them are winning races. Juri Franko, who captured the silver medal at Sarajevo in giant slalom, has a dazzling smile and speaks a number of languages. But he hasn't won a lot of races. On the other hand, Marc Girardelli, who is winning a lot, is quiet and shy. Success in ski racing may be in inverse ratio to how outgoing that racer is.

Also, many ski racers may be socially withdrawn because they come from small mountain towns. Killy, for example, was from Val d'Isère. Stenmark is from Tarnaby, up by the Arctic Circle. We grew up at White Pass, where our only neighbor for a long time was the family who operated the gas station. We were completely isolated.

We were shy even in school. At a high school dance we'd sit along the wall, finding it a great effort to ask a girl to dance. In the seventh grade, for example, we had the choice of square dancing or shoveling snow. We preferred to shovel snow.

Steve felt a painful shyness. "Even as recently as five years ago, I would talk to people only if they asked questions. I wouldn't initiate a conversation.

"Our family was very close, and our strongest relationships were in the home. We were most outgoing when we were involved in sports.

"Although I had a crush on my wife, Debbie, for four years in school, we didn't start going out until our senior year. I had been

A withdrawn Stenmark:
Racers need to place a
protective shield around
themselves.

FRANCISCO MARTINEZ

too shy to ask her for a date. Finally, when I asked her, she said, 'Sure!' I thought to myself, 'What? All this time, and it was as easy as asking!'

"At a ski team fund-raising party, for example—an affair attended by celebrities—I would stand to the side rather than attempt to get to know people—even if it was someone I wanted to meet, like Clint Eastwood."

Not that shyness was on our minds when we left for Europe early in the winter of 1975–76. We were excited, anticipating the Winter Olympics at Innsbruck, Austria, in February.

The Olympics had been in our minds for a long time. In fact, when we first hoped to compete in them, they were to take place in the United States. Denver, Colorado, had won the bid for the 1976 Winter Games, and the new resort at Beaver Creek, near Vail, was to be the site of the Alpine events. It was where we would have skied. But the voters of Colorado rejected the organizers' development plans, and the International Olympic Committee shifted the Winter Olympics to Innsbruck, where the games had been held twelve years earlier.

For Phil the 1975–76 season was an outstanding debut on the international racing circuit. "I moved from the fourth seed in giant slalom, where I was starting way back in the pack, to the first seeded group of racers. By the time the Olympics arrived I was starting with the best fifteen g.s. racers in the world. It took another year before I made first group in slalom.

"It was a revelation at the Olympics, meeting the athletes from the other countries and participating in the ceremonies. Naturally, I was hoping for a medal. But the giant slalom turned out to be another one of those surprise races, won by a tiny wisp of a guy, Heini Hemmi from Switzerland.

"I was an upstart and unknown at the time and came in fifth in the g.s. And the two guys just ahead of me, in bronze and fourth positions, were Ingemar Stenmark and Gustavo Thoeni."

Steve placed thirteenth in the giant slalom. "It turned out to be the best Olympic giant slalom result in my career. You might say I went backward after that. At Lake Placid I was fifteenth, and at Sarajevo, in 1984, I placed seventeenth. It would be laughable, I suppose, except that I won the gold medal in giant slalom at the World Championships in 1982.

"In 1976 I was due to race in the Olympic slalom at Innsbruck. Geoff Bruce was the top-rated American slalom racer, and I was second. But the Innsbruck slalom hill was steep and icy. I wasn't a strong ice skier that early in my career, coming from the Pacific Northwest, where the snow tends to be soft most of the time.

"Like every country at the Olympics, the U.S. was limited to entering just four racers in the event. Geoff Bruce was an automatic. And because Phil had placed fifth in the giant slalom a few days before, there was a feeling the press would tear the U.S. Team apart in print if we didn't enter him in the slalom.

"Then Greg Jones placed reasonably well in the downhill, the opening ski race of the Olympics, so he had a shot at a World Championship combined medal. Even though he didn't have a realistic chance to win a medal in the slalom, it was decided to enter Greg for the combined.

"That left the fourth slot open to either Cary Adgate or myself. I was the automatic, because I was rated higher than Adgate in slalom before going into the Olympics. But I knew I was skiing poorly on ice.

How Olympic Races Are Different (John Fry)

Like all Olympic sports, the Alpine ski events—downhill, slalom, and giant slalom—offer three medals—gold, silver, and bronze—to the top three finishers. Through 1984, in men's and women's events, a total of eighteen Alpine medals were up for grabs.

In regular World Cup races each country is able to enter most of its top competitors in every race. The desirable, early starting positions generally go to the best seeded racers, no matter what country they're from.

The Olympics and World Championships are different. Each nation is limited to four racers in any event. As a result it can happen that a racer in the second seed in a World Cup event may come to start in the first group of fifteen in the Olympics. For example, if Austria has six racers seeded in the first group in downhill, it nevertheless can enter only four in the Olympics. This opens up two earlier starting positions to downhillers from other countries.

Starting after World War II the Federation Internationale de Ski held its World Championships every second winter in even-numbered years. For practical purposes it considered the Winter Olympic races, held quadrennially, to be the World Championships in the years when the Olympics were run. As a result, there was a combined competition in the Olympics, but it was a World Championship Combined, and the medals were not Olympic medals.

Prior to and including the 1980 Winter Olympics, the FIS awarded gold, silver, and bronze medals to competitors who earned the most points based on their combined paper results in the three Alpine disciplines. To be eligible to win a combined medal, a racer had to compete in all three—downhill, slalom, and giant slalom. Billy Kidd won the gold medal in the combined for the United States in 1970, and Greg Jones earned a bronze combined medal at Innsbruck. The last winner of the triple combined was Phil Mahre at Lake Placid.

After 1980 the FIS introduced separate combined races in downhill slalom, and the paper combined was terminated. Starting in 1985, the FIS decided to hold its World Championships in odd-numbered years, and consequently the Olympics no longer count as World Championships.

"I sat down with our coach and said, 'Harald, I'm skiing ice so badly, you should enter Cary.'

" 'Thank you, Steve,' he replied, 'That was what I was hoping you'd say.'

"Cary raced, and Phil and he ended up as the best American men in the slalom. Greg Jones did well enough to win the bronze medal in the World Championship Combined."

Greg had come in eleventh in the spectacular downhill won by Franz Klammer and seen, over and over again, by millions on television. The Austrian ran an amazing race and showed what a great champion he was. In the winters of 1975, '76, and '77 it seemed that no one could beat Klammer in downhill.

We admire him more than any racer we've met over the years. He is an absolutely class act. After 1978 he did poorly and switched brands of skis, never a good idea. But even when he was down he was the same friendly guy he was when he was perched on top of the heap.

Franz never changed character. He was always a happy-go-lucky fellow, always willing to help or give advice. If you were slipping the downhill with him, he'd talk and laugh. When he was losing he never got grumpy or let it get to him. Then he came back and won the downhill World Cup in 1983, four years after his last victory. That's the mark of a true champion. Klammer is someone every racer should look up to.

He suffered a terrible setback when his brother was paralyzed in a downhill accident. But even with that on his mind he managed to make his own comeback and was able to beat the best in the world again.

Franz had his name dragged through the mud, too, for calling Bill Johnson, of the U.S. Team, a "nose-picker." But it was all a misunderstanding. The German or Austrian slang word he used really means a "rookie," or someone who comes out of the pack to win. Franz felt Johnson's first big downhill win at Wengen in 1984 was a result of luck as much as skill, and he said so. But he took a bloodbath in the American press for his remark.

Ingemar, after Innsbruck and the Olympics, where he won only a bronze medal, went on to win the World Cup. Phil placed four-

Austria's Franz Klammer
in 1974: Even when he was
down he was the same
friendly guy. We admired him
more than any other racer.

JOHN FRY

teenth, not bad for his rookie year. For Steve the season was something of a disappointment. "The winter of 1976 was not a good one for me on the World Cup. I earned only twenty-seven points, but I did end the year in the first seed in slalom, so I would have good starting positions the next winter. But it had been my second season on the World Cup, and Phil, in his very first season, had run away from me, winning more than double my number of World Cup points. I planned to quit.

"The 1976–77 World Cup season started, as usual, at Val d'Isère in France. Phil was there, but I didn't go to Europe. Then, bango, I opened the newspaper in Yakima in early December, and there was the headline. Phil had won the first giant slalom race of the World Cup season at Val d'Isère and the first World Cup victory of his career. He was third in the next race.

Phil savors his first World Cup win at Val d'Isère, a giant slalom at the beginning of the 1976–77 season. Even his bib number was right. K2 PHOTO

"Phil called home and said, 'You've got to come back.' So after the Christmas break I returned with him to the World Cup circuit in Europe.

"Still, I hated the travel. Being gone from home bothered me, while Phil seemed to have made the adjustment better.

"After a painful couple of months for me in Europe, the World Cup tour came to the States. At Sun Valley, Phil won the slalom, and I took third. But it hadn't been a good winter. My weight had fallen from 170 pounds almost down to 150. I had no appetite. I was a wreck. My girlfriend, Debbie, and I had broken up at Christmas, and her absence gnawed away at me. In January, when I was in Kitzbühel, I wrote her a letter, but I never mailed it. I threw it in the fireplace. Now I was feeling more strongly than ever my need to get her back. A letter wasn't the way. The only way to do it was to see her in person. My skiing didn't matter anymore.

"After Sun Valley the racers would move on to the next competition, but not me. I said, 'Enough. I'm going home.'

"In the evening, after the slalom race, I asked Phil if I could take his van. I left Sun Valley at 11 P.M. and I drove seven hours straight, all night. I pulled into Yakima about six in the morning, wide awake. I found out that Debbie had a different boyfriend. But I wasn't going to give up. I pursued her, and in a couple of months we were together again.

"Looking back on the affair, I can say now that quitting the World Cup circuit and coming home was the best decision I could have made. Debbie and I were married in 1978, and she's a big part of my life now.

"I'm glad that I came back to skiing too. Although I didn't know it, my better days as a racer were yet to come.

"The next winter I won my first World Cup race at Stratton, Vermont, a slalom. Phil had won the giant slalom the day before, so we managed the first-ever, back-to-back World Cup victories for the United States.

"Phil fell in the slalom at Stratton, but I had the fastest first run. I mean, I was rocketing. All I had to do in the second run was to fend off the dragon slayer, Ingemar. He almost caught me, but I held on

Steve with wife, Debbie, and daughter, Ginger. Quitting the World Cup circuit in 1977 was worth it.

LORI ADAMSKI-PEEK

to my lead and won. The World Cup season was winding down, and what a change it was from Sun Valley the winter before. My confidence was back!"

Confidence, particularly, is learning not to be intimidated by a hill. And intimidation is something every skier must come to grips with. A few weeks before Stratton we were at the World Ski Championships in Garmisch-Partenkirchen, the Bavarian ski resort that is also the site of military R&R facilities for the U.S. Army. We always enjoyed going there because the people are friendly and the place has athletic facilities we can use.

At the '78 Championships, Garmisch lacked snow. There was so little of it, we had to train for the slalom on the landing of the ski jump. The slalom hill itself gave Steve the creeps: "It was very steep, and I didn't care for it. But I surprised myself by coming in eighth,

At Stratton,
Vermont, in 1977,
we had our first
back-to-back
victories. The New
England fans
loved it.

PETER MILLER

After winning the giant slalom at Stratton, Phil fell in the slalom.

PETER MILLER

the best American result. Suddenly the Garmisch slalom hill was transformed in my mind. Now it was one of my *favorite* hills.

"Later, in 1981, I won a World Cup slalom on that hill. Not only was it a favorite, now I felt that no one could beat me on it. I proved it by coming back again in 1982 and winning the World Cup slalom there again, a full second ahead of Phil.

"I learned from that experience not to be intimidated by hills or situations I imagined were conspiring against me.

"Before the winter of 1980–81 I lacked the self-conviction to say, 'I can win any slalom I enter.' It may have been the reason for my previous inconsistency. After that I could say to myself, 'You're as good as anyone on any day, in the world.' "

Phil was starting to find consistency too. "The winter before, I had fallen in a lot of races. Coming into the 1977–78 season, I stood up in five of the first six slaloms and was contending for the World Cup.

"The World Championships at Garmisch were a character builder for me, and they also drew me into international downhill racing, which would ultimately lead to two of the World Cups I would win, in 1981 and 1983.

First taste of big-time downhill came for Phil at Garmisch in 1978. "It was a character builder for me, and later would help me win three World Cups."

"The character building came out of the Garmisch giant slalom and slalom races. In the g.s. I came in fifth, the same as at the Innsbruck Olympics two years before, but this time I was only 19/100ths of a second away from the bronze medal. It slipped out of my grasp in the second run, due to lack of concentration and mental tenacity.

"The bronze medal actually went to the Liechtensteiner, Willi Frommelt. He was a guy who had done nothing all season. Today, if you look up the World Cup results for 1977–78, you won't find Willi Frommelt's name among the first fifty-six finishers. I asked myself, 'How can a guy like that win a medal?' Yet, here he won the bronze at the World Championships by 19/100ths of a second over me, and I would go on to be second in the overall World Cup standings for that winter—on paper, at least, the second-best ski racer in the world.

"It only proves what I've always said, 'A race is only one day in your life,' and Olympic and World Championship medals are often a lottery. There are just certain days when a guy is up for a race, and that must have been Willi Frommelt's day. It wasn't mine.

"In the slalom at Garmisch I fell and was out of the race. The World Championships had been a disaster for me. The rest of the technical—or gate—skiers went home to the States, but because I was in contention for the World Cup I went on to Chamonix in the company of Harald Schoenhaar and our technical rep and ski tuner, Ed Chase.

"The Chamonix slalom was set on a fairly flat hill. I blasted out of the start and recorded the fastest first run. In the second run the pressure was on because Stenmark had already developed a reputation as the best come-from-behind winner in skiing. But I beat him in the second run too. It was a decisive win and, after Garmisch, it built my confidence enormously. I had dominated Stenmark in a race. I came away from Chamonix feeling that I could win any race I entered.

"Suddenly everything turned around for me. I went on to win the giant slalom at Stratton when we got back to the States."

Harald Schoenhaar thinks the Chamonix win may have been one of the most formative experiences in Phil's career.

Coach Schoenhaar was elated by Phil's comeback win at Chamonix in 1978. "Even good athletes have to learn how much it takes for them to win."

PETER MILLER

"It was how he won that was important," Harald says. "He skied a race without mistakes. He attacked from the first gate. Phil had done that in practice before—it was just a matter of time before he did it in actual competition. Even good athletes have to learn, over and over again, how much it takes for them to win."

The 1978 World Championships at Garmisch were important in another respect for Phil: "I began to compete in downhill because I was skiing well enough, perhaps, to get a result in the combined. The following winter, downhill combined results would start to play an important part in winning the overall World Cup.

"It was not an especially promising start. On the Garmisch downhill I was nine seconds out of first place and came in thirty-sixth. Still, if I had stood up in the slalom race later in the championships, I might have won a medal. But I crashed in the slalom, so it was a fruitless exercise. As it happened, fortunately, Pete Patterson won a bronze in the combined for the United States.

"Garmisch was my first real taste of downhill. I can remember feeling so slow. I don't know if we missed the wax, or what.

"There are several reasons why technical, or gate, skiers don't enter downhills. Foremost is the possibility of injury. In slalom or giant slalom I knew that if I fell badly, I might tear up some ligaments, but in downhill a crash could end my career, or it could be bad enough to end my chances for the World Cup in slalom and g.s., where I was good. So in my career I limited my downhill to races that were linked with a slalom or giant slalom to produce combined results.

"The other reason for not competing in downhill is that the practice runs take so much time. This cuts into training time needed for the other two Alpine events.

"I liked the downhill races themselves, but the time needed for training runs, and the tedium of waiting for weather, turned me off. One downhill race can take a whole week out of your schedule— four days of training runs, then the race itself if weather doesn't force a postponement. The time may mean nothing to downhill-only specialists, but if you're running slalom and g.s. also, it creates impossible barriers to success.

"Some of the major downhills were characterized by what we used to call 'the hurry up and wait' syndrome. First, they'd delay the start for a half hour. Then for another half hour. You stood around waiting. Then you hurried to the start only to find the race was being put off for two hours. Then they shut the trail down, and you went back to the hotel. The whole day was wasted.

"It was mentally wearing. Each time you thought you were about to compete, you had to psych yourself for the race. Then it didn't happen. It was frustrating. I found that I had better results when I knew for sure things were going to happen. The changes upset me.

"There's a public misperception that many racers stay away from downhill because they fear the high speeds. That wasn't true of me.

The speed didn't scare me at all. Had it done so, I never would have competed, because fear leads to injury.

"The chances of getting hurt in skiing are increased if you have fear. Fear makes you less aggressive in your skiing, and when you're less aggressive—more passive—you open yourself to falls, accidents, and injuries.

"You also need total concentration to ski, and fear is the enemy of concentration.

"In downhill racing, particularly, there can't be the slightest hesitation in deciding your line. If there's fear in your mind you get behind in thinking about the terrain ahead. And on a high-speed downhill course you have to think ahead all the time.

"Speed is very much a relative thing in skiing, and that's why it's never bothered me. Although you carry a lot of speed in downhill, the distances from one bump, or one gate, to another are often so great that it feels like you're going slowly. You have plenty of time to think about them, compared to turns in slalom.

"I frequently warmed up for downhills by skiing in giant slalom courses on shorter, quicker skis. Everything came at me quickly. Then, when I skied on the downhill course, it felt like everything was slow by comparison. Giant slalom made downhill seem easy.

"There was another funny thing too—if I ran a downhill trail three times without skiing a giant slalom in between, I started to feel the downhill as fast again.

"After I took a couple of training runs each day, in preparing for a downhill competition, I would get to know every little detail and ripple in the course. It actually became repetitious and boring. The challenging thing about slalom and giant slalom is that the courses are always different.

"The mistake most gate skiers make in taking up downhill—and I was guilty of this for a long time—is trying to be too precise in the turns. Instead of letting the skis run, you try to control them. You try to be precise, thinking, 'I've got to be here, I've got to be there.' You hang on too long in the turn, or try to be exactly on line, instead of letting the skis go down the fall line.

"Unlike slaloms, downhills are forgiving. You can be fifteen feet off line and still go fast. In giant slalom you're out of the race if you're that far off line.

"Initially the mistake I made in downhill was in trying to force the skis around, rather than let them come around on their own. In downhill you can be guilty of making too good a turn. The idea should be to *carry speed.* A true downhiller feels the snow. He feels what his skis are doing, he feels whether he's going fast or slowing down. You can't be harsh on the skis.

"A youngster who aspires to be an all-round skier, but who constantly trains slalom, is never going to make it. I was able to ski downhill on the World Cup because, as kids, we skied like crazy down the mountain, going fast. So skiing fast became like second nature. Eventually downhill racing, with its experience of learning how to build speed, and a fresh consciousness of the importance of body positions, helped my giant slalom and slalom. I became better at finding where to pick up speed on a course. I became more aggressive in trying to go faster.

"Every skier, not just a racer, should go out and ski fast at times. Without it your skiing simply won't improve."

The introduction of combined points into the scoring formula in 1978–79 virtually ended Ingemar Stenmark's chances of continuing his string of World Cup victories. Although he tried a downhill once and scored combined points with it, he never attempted it again, and he had to content himself with beating the rest of the world at slalom and giant slalom.

The point formula change, however, laid the groundwork for Phil's domination of the World Cup in the early 1980s. But before that could happen, we would suffer a series of terrible injuries.

PREPARING YOUR SKIS TO SKI, AND CANTING

Even though we had our own tech rep to prepare our skis for racing, we liked—and learned—over the years to do our own ski tuning. Often it was a way to pass a long evening on the tour, and in time we discovered a number of special likes and dislikes in the preparation of our skis.

A well-tuned ski is pretty much essential if you're going to get serious about your skiing. Without a smooth running surface and correctly sharpened and de-burred edges, your skis won't work well and your technique will suffer.

Of course you can have your skis tuned in a ski shop, but the ability to handle the repair and preparation of the skis yourself will give you a better understanding of the tool you have under your foot when you get out on the snow.

For example, if your skis feel grabby or hooky when you go out on the hill in the morning, you will know—if you prepared them yourself—whether the fault is due to having sharpened the steel edges too much at the tip and tail or whether some other factor may be causing the problem.

To tune and wax your own skis you need a few basic hand tools and materials. They include a bastard mill file, a wire brush to clean the filings out of the file, a stone to remove burrs from the steel edges, emery paper to further smooth the edges, and grocery-store plastic steel wool called Scotch-Brite to clean and smooth the polyethylene running surface of the skis.

You'll also need a plastic—not a steel—scraper. Don't use a metal scraper to work the base of the skis. It acts in such a way that it closes the pores in the plastic running surface, and that is something you don't want to do.

To patch holes and gouges in the skis, light a P-Tex candle, purchasable at any ski shop, and drip the material onto the repair areas. After it has hardened, use a body file to remove most of the excess P-Tex. Scrape further with a plastic scraper, then sandpaper and rub with Scotch-Brite.

We advise against using a steel scraper to scrape off excess base material above the level of the steel edges. When we want to take the base down we employ instead sandpaper wrapped around the file, which creates a nice, hard, flat abrasive tool.

In using sandpaper to remove excess plastic base material, choose a coarse—100 to 150—grade paper. If there is a lot of material to remove, we go as coarse as an 80-grade paper.

Sandpaper is handy in other ways. You can use it to rough up the base of the ski. A rough running surface will ski faster on wet snow. The finer the snow, the finer the sandpaper we use.

You can buy a specialized melting device for ski waxing, but it is almost as easy to use an old-fashioned flat laundry iron to melt and drip the wax on the skis. Use your plastic scraper to remove excess wax.

Finally, you'll work a whole lot easier if you spring for a pair of special vises designed specially to hold skis on a workbench.

Sharpening and Smoothing the Edges

Our first step in tuning skis is to see if any of the plastic running surface of the skis is lying above the steel edges. If it is, we work first with sandpaper to bring down the running surface to the level of the steel edges.

Before doing any further work on the bases of the skis, we work on the steel edges. It is important to follow this sequence. If you were to work on the edges after you prepared the softer plastic running surfaces, much of your meticulously done work on the bases could get ruined by the filing and stoning of the edges.

Start by filing the side edge of the ski. We always work with the base of the ski facing away. With the base facing us, we can't file the way we prefer. We like to draw, not push the file, so being right-handed we wind up with the ski facing away, secured by the bench holders.

Ski brakes on your bindings can interfere with filing and scraping the bottoms of the skis and the sides of the edges. Keep sturdy elastic bands handy in your ski-tuning kit and tie the bands around the brake arms in the manner shown here to keep them out of the way when you're working on the skis.

Here's a trick to keep the edge of your plastic scraper sharp at all times. Draw it down the sharp corner of the steel edge to create a smooth scraper with a sharp edge to it. Sand on a hard flat surface to make the scraper edge perfectly straight.

Use a wire brush to keep your file clean at all times.

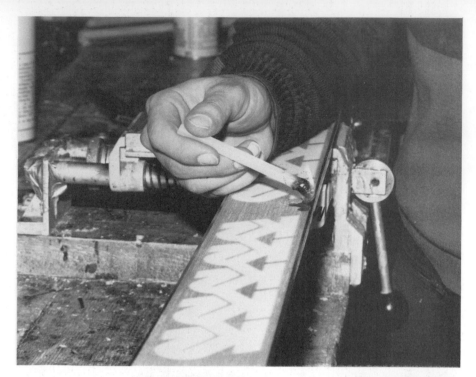

Drip P-Tex repair material into holes and grooves in the polyethylene running surface of the skis. Use a file initially to remove excess repair material.

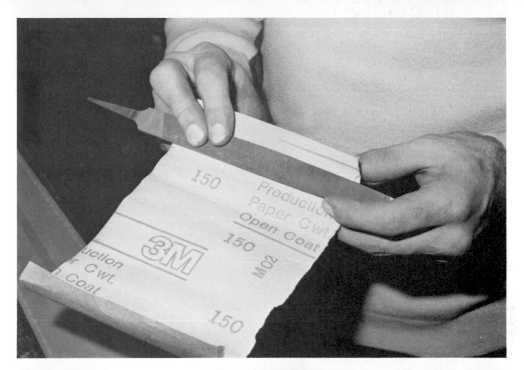

To remove any plastic running surface lying above the level of the steel edges, wrap sandpaper around the file, then bring down the undesired areas with the sandpaper.

At left, the correct way to bottom-file the edges. If you file incorrectly, (below), the edges will not be sharpened square. Flat-file before and after side-filing the edges.

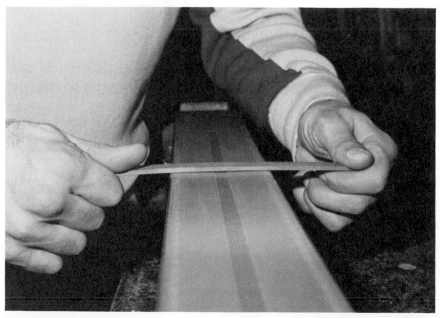

To file the side edge of the ski, draw the file down the ski (with the running surface of the ski facing away from you if you are right-handed). Remove all burrs and nicks in the edges as you sharpen. Edge filing is done when you can see that all the steel along the edge is shining.

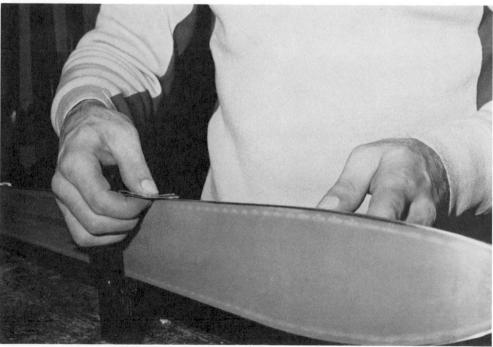

Further refine your edge work, first with a stone to remove any burrs still left after filing, and then with emery paper.

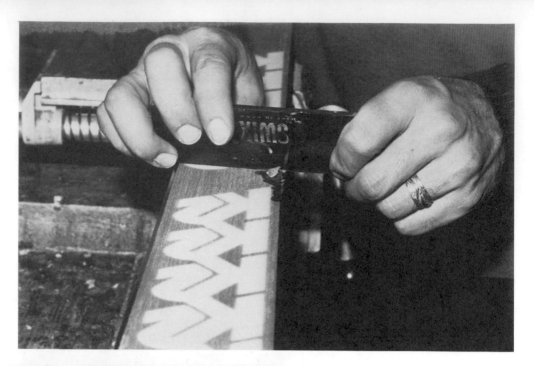

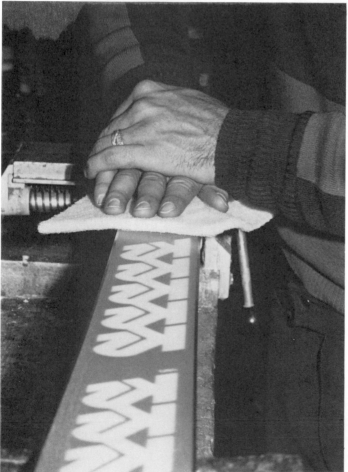

After filing the steel edges, work to obtain a perfectly smooth bottom. Use a plastic scraper to remove excess plastic base material in order to make the running surface of the ski perfectly flush with the edges. A further smoothing is done with a plastic steel-wool pad. Avoid using a steel scraper. The aim is to open up the pores in the ski to receive the wax.

We like to work from left to right. When we are working one edge, we work from the tip to the tail. To do the other edge, we turn the ski over and work from the tail to the tip.

When we come to a spot where the steel edge is hardened or nicked, we work it vigorously back and forth with the file. Periodically we rub the file with the wire brush to clean out of its grooves the filings from the steel edges.

After filing the edges, side and bottom, we rub a fine-grained stone down the edges to remove any burrs. Then we smooth the edges further with emery paper, which we fold into four layers to make it stiff so it can be applied squarely to the edge. The emery paper supplies an even smoother finish than the stone.

For giant slalom racing, more than slalom, we also use the emery paper to dull the steel edges in the areas of the tips and tails of the skis. Actually, before a g.s. race, we used to arrive at the hill with the edges only slightly dulled. We'd then test the snow and do further dulling until the skis felt right. Sometimes we dulled only ten inches or so of edge in front and back; other times we'd dull as much as two thirds the length of the ski, leaving just the area under the boots sharp as a razor.

The harder the snow, the longer the length of sharpened edge you need. The softer the snow, the farther back you dull. Too sharp an edge in soft snow will cause the ski to grab excessively.

A rule of thumb we used was that if you dull the tail by a foot in length, then you should probably dull the edge in the tip area by a foot and a half. A lot of the time when we raced, most of our weight was toward the tail of the ski. If we dulled the tail the same length as the tip, we'd have too much edginess in the tail relative to the tip of the ski.

Waxing

We prefer the system of melting the wax and dripping it on the skis, then using a flat hot iron to smooth the wax uniformly over the skis' running surface. You can do this with a specialized combined wax melter and iron that allows you to mix different waxes carefully

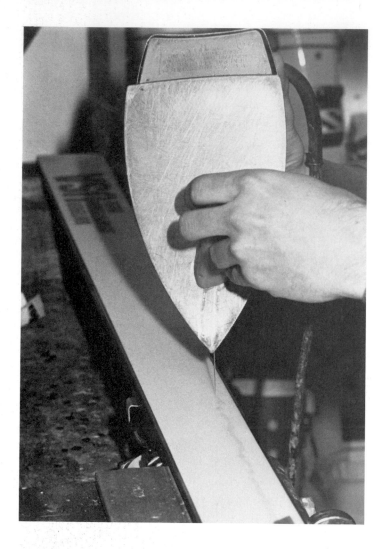

Set the iron at a moderate temperature and drip wax onto the running surface of the ski on either side of the groove. After dripping on the wax, iron it smooth, then let the ski stand for fifteen minutes to allow the warm wax to be absorbed into the plastic running surface.

by measure, available in most ski specialty shops, but for most people it's sufficient to own an old-fashioned flat laundry iron. Steer clear of steam irons with holes in them; the holes will retain wax and dirt from prior waxings and release part of the material into your new wax job.

With the specialized ski-waxing device, you can mix waxes more precisely. Say the snow conditions are such that you'd want to mix two parts of red to one part yellow. You open up the device and drop in two red wax bars and one yellow. That would give you a perfect mix. The wax melts under the electricity and drips out of the two holes in the appliance on either side of the groove as you run it down the length of the ski. You can do almost the same thing by holding the two bars of wax against a regular hot iron.

Do not wax skis immediately after bringing them in from the outdoors. Allow several hours for the skis to warm up to room temperature.

In waxing, be careful not to overheat the wax. If you see it smoking or turning white on the ski, cease waxing until the iron has cooled off. Overheated wax will lose some of its ingredients to the air—ingredients you want to get into the base of the ski. Use moderation: don't wax too hot or too cold. If you're using a laundry iron, set it for "rayon."

Before flat-scraping the wax off the base, we like to remove wax on the edges and any drippings on the sidewalls of the skis. Use the groove scraper to remove wax from the groove. Then use the plastic scraper to flat-scrape the base. Finally, finish up by removing the last excess wax with the Scotch-Brite cloth or pad. Good smooth base, good smooth finish, and you're ready to go skiing with the easiest turns you'll ever make.

One trick we use is to clean out the pores of the skis' running surface with a first waxing. Apply yellow wax to the base and, before it has a chance to cool, apply the plastic scraper, vigorously drawing it down the running surface of the ski to remove as much of the wax as possible. By scraping in this manner when the wax is still warm, you'll actually pull old wax and dirt out of the pores in the plastic base, wax that you don't want there, and more of your new wax will get into the ski for the conditions of the day. It's a way to clean the base of the skis, preparatory to final waxing, and we prefer it to using a solvent wax cleaner.

For the final waxing it's a good idea to apply the hot wax, iron it smooth, then allow ten to fifteen minutes for it to get absorbed into the plastic running surface of the ski before you start scraping. Do *not* take the ski outdoors and allow it to get cold before scraping. You'll only cause the wax to chip and flake when you scrape.

This modern wax melter and iron allows easy mixing of waxes for varying snow conditions.

Scrape all excess wax off the running surface with vigorous use of the plastic scraper. The only wax you want on the ski is that which has been absorbed into the running surface.

As a final step before skiing, use emery paper at a 45-degree angle to dull the edges at the tips and tails of the skis. The softer the snow, the longer the edge section being dulled. Keep the edge portion under the foot as sharp as possible at all times.

Waxing for Racing

Waxing is most critical, of course, in downhill races. The downhillers in Europe typically impregnate the bottoms of their skis with yellow wax, anticipating warmer temperatures at the bottom of the course. Then they wax for the flattest, longest sections on top. If it's colder high on the course, they may surface-wax with red. By the time they reach the bottom of the run, their skis have lost the red and they're skiing on yellow.

Wax for the flat sections of the courses, not for the steep. A ski will usually run well on the steep part of any hill, no matter what the wax. But on the flats a bad wax can lose you the race.

Because World Cup slalom races are so icy, wax is unimportant in these events. Usually, in slalom, we just raced on the bases impregnated with yellow wax.

In giant slalom we melted yellow, or a mix of yellow and red, into the base. And as in downhill, there was the added complexity of using hardeners to cope with different kinds of snow crystallization.

Our technical rep, Ed Chase, did almost all our waxing over the years. In general the tech reps like Chase stay in close touch with the wax manufacturers and follow their charts.

Waxing for Recreational Skiing

Many recreational skiers who expect to be skiing all day think that, unlike racers, they should apply more wax to make it last through several hours of skiing. This is a mistake. The additional wax will simply allow scratches and grooves to form on the running surface, slowing the ski and making it harder to turn.

The recreational skier's waxing goal should be the same as the racer's: to get as much of the wax as possible soaked into the plastic pores of the base and create a perfect smooth surface for skiing. To do this you need to create, with plastic scraper and sandpaper, the underlying conditions in the plastic base of the ski so that it can absorb the wax—doing it with the techniques we have described here. When you're ironing you can usually tell the areas where the P-Tex is dry and needs wax.

We recommend that everyone try to wax their skis once a week during the winter. It's also good to wax before transporting the skis and storing them over the summer. In this case you simply want to apply the wax all over the base and the edges to protect them from dirt and moisture. When winter comes again, or you arrive at your destination, scrape off all the wax and prepare the skis for skiing again.

Also, it's a good idea, when transporting skis in a bag, to put cardboard between the running surfaces at the tips and tails and strap them together securely. This will keep the edges and bases from rubbing together and getting damaged.

If it's raining outside, or there's slush and salt on the roads, do not transport the skis exposed on a roof rack. Your edges and bindings will be damaged. Carry them inside the car or have a rack to which the whole ski bag can be strapped. When you get home after a day of skiing, it's also a good idea to dry the skis and bindings with an old towel.

Can You or Cant You?

One of the principal aims of ski boot design—in addition to making your foot comfortable when you ski—is to enable you to pressure the inside edge of the ski in a turn. Being able to get quickly on edge is what you need to make the ski carve, skid, and stop efficiently. You do this by a lateral action of your ankle and lower leg. These extremities form the shaft of the steering wheel.

The link between lower leg steering and the steel edge of the ski is the boot. Without a well-designed boot, it is difficult to control the edges of the skis.

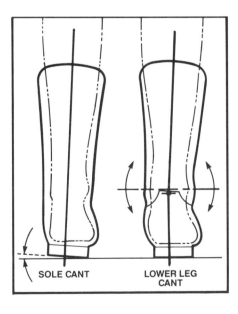

SOLE CANT   LOWER LEG
                   CANT

People's legs and feet are configured differently. Some people are bowlegged, and their lower leg has a slight outward arch. Other folks may be knock-kneed. The former configuration is more common, to the point where many such people are prone to walk on the outside of their feet. When it comes to skiing they need help in the form of an adjustment in the boot. They need something that will enable them to ride a perfectly flat ski rather than ride on the outside edges of the skis, something that will allow them to move their leg less distance to the inside in order to edge the ski.

There are two schools of thought about how to bring about this correction. One school advocates raising the sole of the boot along its inside edge, actually angling it to the top of the ski. This has the effect, somewhat, of changing how a person skis. Warren Witherell, a prominent coach and technique author, has advocated a similar approach. We think it's wrong.

You shouldn't change how a person skis by canting the whole boot. Rather, the sole of the foot should be flat on the ski. The cant, or angle, should be in the upper boot, and its only purpose should be to accommodate the individual morphology of the skier.

The aim of canting should not be to change the angle of the foot's sole to the ski; rather, the upper boot should be adjusted to fit the particular angle of the skier's lower leg.

Our feet sit on a totally flat bed within the boot. The canting is done from the riveted-on upper cuff of the boot, on up. Our cuffs are canted about three degrees. We don't grind the sole of the boot or affect its flatness in any way. Some racers experiment with applying duct tape between the boot and the ski. Then their bindings usually don't work properly. If you're going to cant, do it within the boot. If you want more edging power temporarily, you can place a bit of padding between the inside of the lower shin and the boot interior. Or if you're not worried about riding a perfectly flat ski all the time, you can adjust the outward tilt of the upper boot a notch more to increase the pressure on the inside of the lower leg.

If you have too much cant the ski will roll up and try to turn tighter than you want. The ski will snake. If you don't have enough cant you can edge as hard as you can and you'll still feel that you don't have enough edging power. You'll slide.

The cant of our boots is about standard for most boots that come off the shelf and are bought by recreational skiers. Most of the boots sold today have a mechanical device that will allow you to adjust the cant of the cuff to your leg, or the ski shop can do it for you.

We can tell if a boot is right for us—or if it is going to make it hard to get easily from one edge to the other—just by putting it on and rolling it on the hard floor with ankle motion. Six years ago we started with zero cant, then gradually moved up to three degrees.

Racers tend to want boots with more forward lean than most recreational skiers would feel comfortable with. Steve has 21 degrees forward lean, Phil 19 degrees. Recreational skiers will want a lean of between 16 and 18 in the boots they buy.

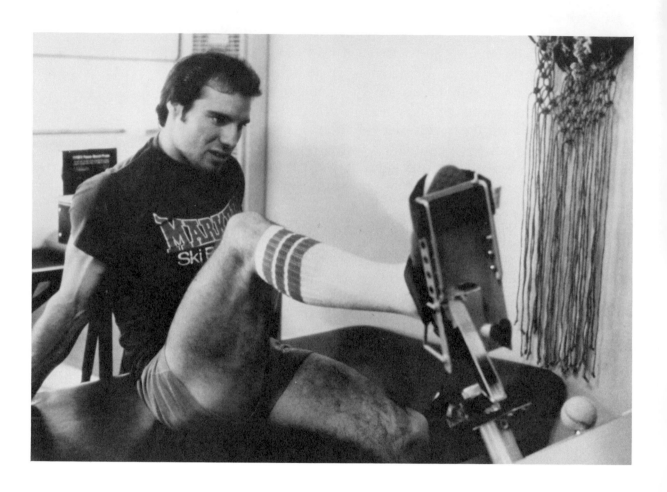

SIX

MODERN MEDICINE AT WORK

Injury is part of the sport of skiing, but you always ski with the belief it's never going to happen to you. So you don't fear injury. People who say that fear of injury deters people from skiing don't know what they're talking about.

Fear of steepness, speed, or of a certain trail is a mental thing in skiing. Once, at Garmisch-Partenkirchen, a major stop on the World Cup tour, Steve was definitely frightened of a certain section of the downhill:

"Sure enough, that's where I crashed. But I wasn't injured, and the fall got the fear out of my system. On the next training run I was fine. Like falling off a horse, you have to get back on and drive the fear out."

Fear normally has never bothered us, but when we first saw the Hahnenkamm downhill at Kitzbühel, in Austria, we thought, "No way. A person would have to be half-crazy to ski this."

The Hahnenkamm is by far the most fearsome downhill in the world. In the starting gate your heart has to be doing 150. You're wired.

From the start you pole out, skate twice to build speed, then get in a tuck. After eight seconds your speed feels like it's nearing maximum, yet the trail becomes steeper. It's mind-boggling.

Phil in the downhill: "People who say that fear of injury deters people from skiing don't know what they're talking about." TEAM RUSSELL

There's no time to prepare for all the things you have to overcome. The trail seemingly has no place to glide or relax, to let you gather yourself for what's ahead. You're into speed from the start, and it just keeps coming.

The famous Steilhang is so steep that you can't even see the protective netting below, and it's easy to panic when you can't see something you know is there.

On the road it's time to concentrate on riding a flat ski and on holding a good tuck position. The traverse is a sidehill and very fast. After that you make a couple of turns, you glide for just a moment, then suddenly you're at the Hausberg jump, followed by a compression turn.

A compression is when you go from a steep face to a relative flat area, and the force pushes your knees up into your face. Greg Jones once did a helicopter on the Hausberg. He actually spun full circle and continued down the trail at full tilt. Steve did it once too. As his tips came around, though, one hit the snow and the ski came off. He crashed.

After the Hausberg there's a steep traverse, and you have to fight to hold a line to the next gate. On the last pitch, in January when the Hahnenkamm is always held, the light is flat, it's hard to feel the terrain, and you have to deal with another compression before the finish. It's some kind of ski trail, right to the end.

After our first experiences of the Hahnenkamm, fear simply turned to respect. If there was any lingering fear, it wasn't for the course itself, but for the possibility of a fall causing an injury which would take us out of the technical ski events—slalom and giant slalom—where we could win races.

When the injuries did come, they weren't a result of downhill. Worse, they came like a plague. The year of 1979 was when it happened. It was terrible, and were it not for one doctor, it's doubtful if either of us would have gone on to Olympic, World Championship, and World Cup medals.

Steve

In the spring of 1979 I damaged some cartilage in my knee in a dirt-bike accident. Immediately I went to see Dr. Richard Steadman in South Lake Tahoe, California.

We had met Dick Steadman when we first joined the ski team. He was the team physician and a specialist in lower leg injuries. He invited us to his clinic, not far from the Heavenly Valley ski area, to be tested. We remember something odd: he remarked on the tightness of our knees, more pronounced than in most ski racers. It was true.

People who ski frequently necessarily employ a lot of lateral knee angulation over the years in edging their skis. It is by no means a natural body motion, since the knee is designed to flex forward, not sideways. For that reason, it's believed, skiers develop loose knee ligaments. Anyway, Steadman seemed impressed that our knees were still tight after years of hard skiing.

Knee and ankle magician Dr. Dick Steadman celebrates the results of his surgery at the Sarajevo Olympics. *SKI* MAGAZINE

Dick Steadman is not only a remarkable surgeon, he took a remarkable interest in us as people. After each of his operations he would take us out of the hospital and have us stay in his home, where he could work directly on rehabilitating the leg.

To cope with my bike injury Steadman removed some cartilage. He gave me a big Lenox Hill brace to wear on the right knee when I skied—the kind professional football players use after they've been injured. I wore it for several years, along with a lighter brace on the left knee.

After recovering from the bike injury, in December of 1979 I raced in a downhill at Val Gardena in Italy. I went off a bump, hit a ball of ice, and my skis crossed. I felt like I was falling at 400 miles an hour. My bindings released, and my body was sliding hard on the snow. I saw the protective fence coming up. "It'll save me from being injured," I thought. I was loose, lying flat, and relaxed.

But the fence didn't hold me. It just flopped over. I kept sliding into the woods, going fast. Finally, I wrapped around a tree and broke two ribs.

After they hauled me out of the woods the doctors who examined me feared that I might have ruptured my spleen, so they put me on hold. I went back to the States to let the ribs heal.

In January 1980 we returned to Europe, and in the first race I hooked a tip on a slalom pole. It tore two ligaments in my right ankle—the same leg I had injured on my dirt bike the previous spring.

The German doctor said I'd be fine in a week, it was just a sprain. After seven days, though, I still couldn't put a boot on my foot.

We traveled from Kitzbühel to Wengen. Three more days passed, and there was still no improvement. So I called Dick Steadman. I explained the situation to him. Immediately he said, "I know just what it is. Come home. It's going to take six to eight weeks."

A football player's knee brace kept Steve racing, but the injuries came like a plague.
TEAM RUSSELL

Steadman knew just by our conversation on the transatlantic phone what was the matter with me, yet I hadn't been able to get a correct diagnosis in Europe.

Many of the top European racers, when they're injured, come to South Lake Tahoe to see Steadman. In turn he tries to go to Europe at the beginning of each season to make sure that everyone— mostly the U.S. racers—who suffered injuries the previous season is okay and has rehabbed well. He has become a kind of doctor to the international ski-racing world. He treated Irene Epple of the German ski team. His most notable achievement was to put Marc Girardelli together. Girardelli tore all four ligaments in his knee when it twisted around 180 degrees in a fall.

Based on my phone call to Steadman, I flew from Europe to South Lake Tahoe, and we started work immediately on the injured ankle. The Olympics were only a month away. I had wasted ten days in Europe when I should have been doing rehab. It looked like I might miss Lake Placid.

Phil

Lake Placid had been my undoing the previous winter. In February 1979 I took a fall there that was shown on reruns during the Olympics in 1980. They played the videotape over and over, saying, "Look at this guy. Only a year ago he took this fall, and now he's racing in the Olympics!" No wonder the public gets strange ideas about skiing.

The 1979 pre-Olympic accident couldn't have happened at a worse time. The combined had been introduced into the World Cup, and I was coming into my own. I had finished second in the World Cup the year before, and now I had a real shot at winning it.

Peter Luescher of Switzerland was leading, but he couldn't earn any more points in giant slalom unless he won a race. On the other hand, I was wide open to win points.

In the first run of the giant slalom at Lake Placid I came to a midpoint on the course where there was a little pitch. I was a trifle low in my line, but I knew that the course became straighter below, so I figured I could recapture the correct line of descent when I reached there.

But I hadn't figured on the closed gate. A closed gate in slalom or giant slalom is one that is not open to your line of approach, but rather one pole of the gate is set directly behind the other in the line of your attack.

I came into the turn low and hit the downhill pole. My left ski scraped against it, and then it hooked on to the toepiece of my binding. It caught violently, twisting my leg and pitching me over my tips.

I knew I'd broken the leg before I even hit the snow, because I'd broken my other leg twice before. What hurt more than the pain, though, was the knowledge that my season was finished, the dream of the World Cup ended again. Mentally, it was a killer.

They took me down on the toboggan and cut my giant slalom suit off me. The examining doctor said it looked bad, a complicated break. At the hospital in Lake Placid they said an operation would be needed.

In seeking a specialist to perform the operation they called Dick Steadman, who told them he had experienced success in dealing with my particular fracture. The next day John McMillian, a wealthy Salt Lake businessman, who is a trustee of the U.S. Ski Team, flew me in his own jet direct to South Lake Tahoe.

The operation took four hours and entailed the insertion of a plate and seven screws. After the surgery I was placed in the hospital near Heavenly Valley, where the World Cup racers had come after Lake Placid.

Newspaper and television reporters were besieging me for interviews, so the team called a press conference. Dick Steadman and Hank Tauber were there. Steadman described for the press the complexity and seriousness of my leg injury. It was the first time I heard how close I had come to having an injury that would have ended my career.

Strange as it seems now, something happened at the press conference that caused everyone to laugh. Serge Lang asked Dr. Steadman if I would be able to ski with the screws in my ankle.

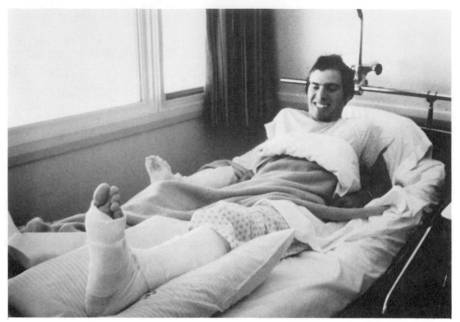

Phil's fracture at Lake Placid nearly ended his career. Rehab started only six hours after surgery. MERRILYN M. BROWN

"Yes," Steadman said without thinking, "Phil will be able to screw with the skis in his ankle."

Clearly, though, I had been through a traumatic experience. I was white as a ghost. My mother, who was there, urged me to go back to the hospital and not try to watch the races.

A few of the racers—my teammates and Andy Wenzel, who would win the World Cup the following season—visited me in the hospital. But I was depressed by the fact that so many of the other racers who were at Heavenly Valley didn't come to see me. Even when I went out to the finish area and sat in the sun watching the racers come down, few of them came over to talk to me. Maybe they thought I was a jinx, that coming in touch with me would give them bad luck.

A week after surgery Dick Steadman moved me out of the hospital into his home. Each morning, before he went to his clinic, he worked on my leg and showed me the exercises I should use in my rehab. He put me in a removable splint, one that I could take off for my exercises.

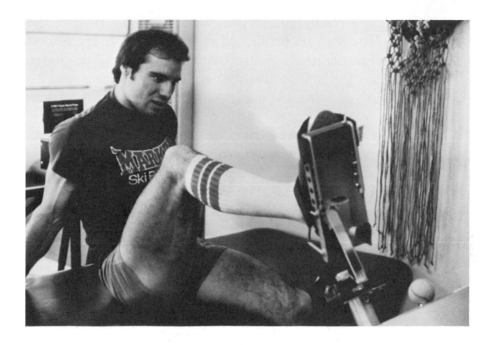

Steadman works with Phil on resistance exercises at his clinic at Lake Tahoe.

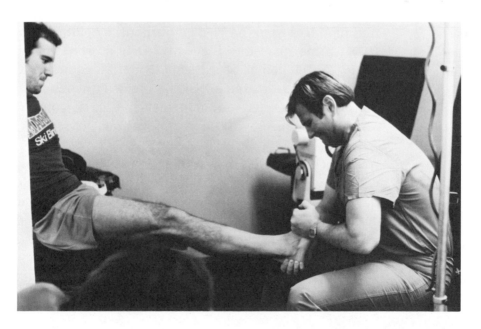

The rehab actually started just six hours after the surgery. At first it was simple flexing of the ankle and wriggling the toes. The break had been in the joint, so the idea of the movement was to keep the weight-bearing surfaces in the joint smooth. In the evening Dick would come back to his house and work with me some more.

He is a remarkable doctor. Once at Sun Valley, in 1977, I experienced severe back pain in a race. I bent down after the first run to release my bindings and I could hardly stand up. Dick Steadman was there, and I told him I needed to race the second run in order to retain my national giant slalom title.

Immediately Steadman began to ice my back with snow. He forced me to do sit-ups. Then he iced the back some more. Then more exercises. He kept my back frigid and exercised until the last possible moment before I was due in the starting gate. It was the craziest treatment I'd ever experienced, but I guess it worked. I raced, oblivious to the pain because I was concentrating so hard on the course. I won the race and kept my title, but at the finish the pain was again horrible. I was barely able to walk for the next three days.

After my 1979 recuperation at Steadman's place, I went home to Yakima. I had been married eight months before, in the summer of 1978—a month before Steve and Debbie were married—to Paula Davis, a high school sweetheart. She had come to Steadman's in Lake Tahoe to be with me, but she seemed uncomfortable there and went home. Actually our marriage had been going on the rocks from the beginning, and now the leg fracture simply added to the burden.

Steven still doesn't understand why Paula and I married at all.

"They were together and apart so many times before the marriage, I lost count. She may have been only seventeen when he married her, just out of high school. Though I thought the marriage wouldn't work, I wasn't about to tell him to get his stuff together and forget about it."

We had gone to West Yellowstone for our honeymoon and immediately proceeded to argue. For her the past was still the present: past girlfriends, past relationships. There was intense jealousy.

We cut the honeymoon short and went home, but we continued to fight on the trip back. We'd argue about simple things, like whether to fly or drive. Glasses of milk were thrown at dinner. We'd fight in the middle of the night.

That summer of 1979, when I was still recovering from the leg break, I spent a lot of time at Steven's, working on a buggy. Paula said that if I was going to spend all my time at Steven's during the day, she was going to spend all her time at night with her friends. So for a week, every night, she stayed out till five in the morning.

It was a doozy of a marriage. At the time I felt that she was to blame, but marriage obviously is a two-way street, so I can't put all the blame on her. I guess we were too immature to be married or to understand what the vows of marriage meant.

One day I said, "That's it." I took off for a week, came home, and said, "I'm done. I'm leaving. I'm history." A few months later we were divorced.

Meanwhile, I kept at work, rehabbing my leg. I had purchased an exercise bicycle and I pedaled on it with my good leg. I needed to raise my heart rate to pump blood into the healing zone. And seven times a day I'd remove the splint and exercise the ankle of the injured leg.

Five weeks after the operation I began resistance exercises. I needed a partner to supply the resistance, but in those last days of my marriage the partner wasn't very willing to work with me on it. So I did it on my own.

I took an old bicycle inner tube, placed it around the bottom of my foot, and pulled up and down against my toes, flexing the ankle. By the end of the sixth week I was able to go out and ride my ten-speed bike.

I started to bike on an uphill and downhill circuit, ten miles a day. I did that for several weeks, then was able to begin weight-bearing, adding ten pounds a week. Week by week I measured the added pressure I could put on a scale.

Finally, I could walk, but there were times, with my marriage and all, when I asked myself whether it was worth what I was doing just to stay in ski racing. I thought about quitting. "What do I have to prove?" I asked myself. Deep down, though, I found a desire to come back, to prove myself.

In July I skied for the first time at Mount Hood outside of Portland, Oregon. I wondered if the leg would hold up. Somehow I think broken legs become stronger than they were before. Nevertheless, my ski boot hurt me and I knew that some screws would have to come out of my leg if I was going to race.

In August I trained with the ski team in Australia, mainly free skiing. Quickly I was getting back into the swing of things. When I returned to the States I had three of the screws removed from my ankle.

Although I would feel some pain in my leg at Lake Placid, I was back on skis and racing again. I give all the credit to Dick Steadman. Without him my silver medal at Lake Placid, the three World Cups, and the gold medal at Sarajevo would not have been possible.

At Lake Placid I competed in the opening downhill race. Considering what I was coming back from, entering the Olympic downhill may have looked to some like a foolish risk. It wasn't. I fell only twice in downhills in my career, without serious injury.

Once, at Chamonix, near the Mont Blanc in France, I crossed my tips, fell, and slid 150 yards. The other time was at Val Gardena, in the Italian Dolomites on the World Championship downhill course, where I caught an edge and fell flat on my face. The snow was soft, but it rung my bell anyway. I've seen others take brain-rattling falls that would probably have caused me to abandon downhill. Fortunately that hadn't happened to me, so here I was in the Lake Placid downhill.

Many racers and coaches were critical of the Whiteface Mountain course, which, while steep on top, was entirely too flat on the bottom to be called a true Olympic challenge. I had no complaints, though. I had a good run, one of the best results of my downhill career. I placed fourteenth, which, normally, would rank me with

The payoff: A silver medal in the slalom at the 1980 Lake Placid Olympics.
K2 PHOTO

the first seeded group in downhill in the world. Already I was in great shape to win the FIS Combined.

The Olympic giant slalom hill at Whiteface Mountain, by contrast, is one of the better competition slopes in the world. The most that can be said of my run on it, however, is that I stood up with a respectable tenth place. Stenmark won his first Olympic gold medal.

The slalom is traditionally held on the last day of the Olympics, and, apart from the continuing discomfort in my ankle, I was in great shape, having been handed starting bib number 1. There was a fresh dusting of snow on the course and I had ideal conditions to ski on, running first. I ended up with the fastest first-run time, a half second over Jacques Luethy, the Swiss slalom star, and Stenmark.

In the second run the first five racers start in the reverse order of their finishing results from the first run. Therefore I would be at something of a disadvantage starting fifth, with Luethy and Stenmark enjoying slightly better snow ahead of me.

My run down the second course was not what you'd call vintage skiing. A half-dozen times I found myself low on the gates, or off my outside ski too early in the turns. A slalom pole came out of the snow and slipped between my legs, which hurt my concentration. At the finish I was 1.08 seconds slower than Stenmark.

My time for the two runs was good enough, however, to beat Luethy (bronze) and win the silver medal, the first Olympic medal won by an American male in Alpine skiing since Bill Kidd and Jimmy Heuga in 1964. And I won the FIS gold medal in the combined.

Steve

A week before the Olympics I began skiing again. At first I just free-skied, hardly training at all in the gates. I avoided any rutted courses that might hurt my leg. I was in pain, but I was determined to race.

Because of the lack of snow at Lake Placid, hill space to train there was scarce, so the U.S. Team trained and stayed at Killington, Vermont. A Bell helicopter took us back and forth to the races, from the Green Mountains to the Adirondacks, fourteen of us at a time. We were Olympic commuters.

At the opening ceremonies we suffered the same transportation snafu that caused so much discomfort to spectators at the games. The road back to town was jammed with people, and there was no room for the buses to move. We walked most of the way.

All I could do to relieve the pain in my ankle was to pack it with ice at the end of the day. Between runs I had to unbuckle the boot. In skiing there's no point in taking Novocain to freeze the injured area. If you desensitize an injured skier's foot he isn't able to feel the snow or the pressure of the ski edging. About all you can do is take strong analgesics, which may help reduce the swelling too.

I placed fifteenth in the giant slalom. Then in the slalom a pole got under my feet at the sixth gate and I was out. It was not a great Olympics. But at least, by the end of that season, I was skiing well again. I had one more knee operation in 1980, then the days of doctors and icepacks were over for a while.

In 1982, Dick Steadman would operate on me again—first in December of that winter and again in March after I hurt a knee playing basketball. After the December operation I won the giant slalom gold medal in the World Championships. Eleven days after the second operation, in March, I won a race that enabled me to finish third in the overall World Cup behind Phil and Ingemar Stenmark. That's some kind of doctoring.

In the winter of 1985, Steadman operated again on my knees, but this time, with my racing days behind me, I stayed on crutches for almost two months.

The injuries became forgotten. I just decided that they were the last that I would have, and I still ski believing that there is no possibility of getting hurt. In ski racing, if you fear injury, you won't go fast enough to win.

THE TACTICS OF SKIING

So far in these instruction sections of this book we have talked about ski technique. We have shown *how* to turn. Now we'll talk about *where* to turn. From technique we go to tactics.

When we walk on the street the movements of walking—learned long ago and completely integrated into our unconscious—are automatic. We're no longer concerned about how to walk but where we are going, where to turn at what corner, and when to stop at the curb for traffic.

Similarly, in skiing, technique—the edging of the skis, the independent leg movements, the initiation and steering of turns—should become so automatic that we don't have to think about how to make a turn. Rather, we can concentrate on the tactics of when and where to turn to realize the optimal line of descent down the hill.

The ideal tactical training for any skier—even for a recreational skier who has no serious intention of becoming a racer—is to ski through gates. Unlike free skiing, coming down through a series of gates forces you to make a turn in a specific place. The skier who learns to ski gates can ski anywhere, because he or she has undergone the discipline of making a turn where it is absolutely necessary. Such a skier skis more safely and in better control. Moreover, the discipline of running gates forces the skier to ski technically well. There is no room for sloppy, windshield-wiper turns, or for lack of up-and-down motion to start and finish the turn, when it has to be made at a certain place and time. Tactics reinforce good technique.

The purpose of this section is not to insist that the only worthwhile skiing is done in gates. On the contrary, every skier—including the top racer—needs a lot of free skiing as well. Racers who ski only in the gates eventually suffer from too much control and edging in their skiing and lose the feel for gliding.

You assimilate technique by hundreds of miles of free skiing. In gate skiing you marry your technique to tactics.

Long Turns, and Where to Make the Turn

Here is a typical setting of gates for a giant slalom, or NASTAR-type course. The poles are set in such a way that the skier must go back and forth across the hill.

There is a right place, and a wrong place, to make the turn. For training purposes here, we use a marker in the snow to indicate to the skier where the turn should be made.

Specifically, the marker is set in the snow directly above the inside pole of the gate, in a line with the fall line of the hill. It is placed along that line so that, as the skier crosses the hill, the marker also lines up with the outside pole of the next gate.

The best way to get a feeling for where to make the turn is to start out slowly, in a snowplow. The idea is to begin the turn before reaching the marker. In this way the skis already are pointed downhill before the skier reaches the gate.

Long Turns, Tactics, and Line

Here is the same setting of gates, but the skier is moving at higher speed. On the top gate the skier is already pointed downhill before reaching the inside pole, and the turn is mostly completed as he rounds the pole.

Coming across the hill, the skier directs his skis at the outside pole of the next gate. This is the correct approach in skiing long-turn, wide-set gates in slalom or giant slalom.

Approaching the marker set vertically above the inside pole of the next gate (to indicate where the skier should turn), he initiates the turn and begins to steer it around the marker, *not* around the pole of the gate.

By the time he reaches the inside pole of the gate the turn is mostly completed and the skier is heading, again, for the outside pole of the next gate.

The old rule in gate skiing was to turn high. But turning high isn't always correct, as we will discuss later. The new rule when turning through a succession of long turn gates is to direct the skis at the outside pole of each gate. The result—turning high—is the same, but the rule is different.

Wrong Line, Wrong Technique

Even though the gate setting here is simple—and in some ways similar to free skiing on an open hill—there is plenty of room for skiers to make errors.

In the first sequence (A) the skier comes out of the top gate and fails to aim his skis at the outside pole of the next gate. Rather than steering his turn around the marker, he initiates the turn inside the marker and steers around the inside pole of the gate. As a result he comes through the last gate with his skis not yet fully turned. He won't be able to line up correctly with the next gate unless he makes a massive lateral move and a slowing uphill glide to regain a good line.

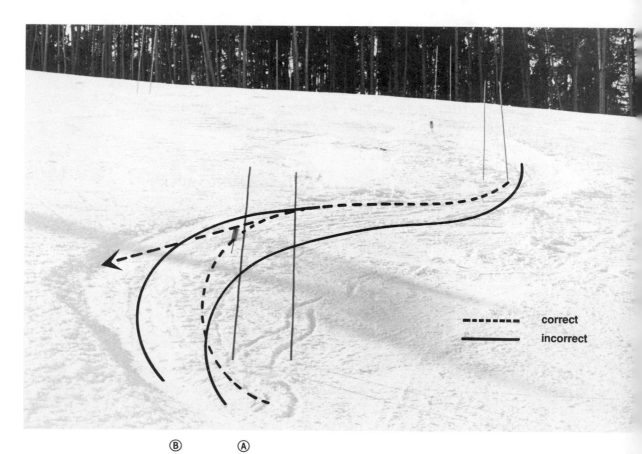

- - - - - - -   correct
——————   incorrect

Ⓑ   Ⓐ

ILLUSTRATION A

ILLUSTRATION B

In this sequence (B) the skier lacks technique as much as good line. Note the absence of definitive up-and-down motion as he turns. In the preparation phase his body is not compressed and creates no springboard to propel him into the turn. This lack of body dynamic results in a weakly edged outside ski, which tends to skid around the marker. There is no carving action, and by the time he reaches the inside pole of the gate, he will be considerably downhill from it. Lack of technique causes lack of line.

Long Slalom Turns

On the previous pages we showed the correct line for skiing long turns in giant slalom. The principle is the same for slalom. Here the gates are set laterally apart, requiring the skier again to ski back and forth across the hill. The only difference is that the gates are set somewhat tighter—that is, closer together down the hill.

As in giant slalom, the slalom skier, in approaching the next gate, directs his skis at its outside pole. The turn is made around the marker and virtually completed as the skier rounds the inside pole of the gate, enabling him to direct his skis at the outside pole of the next gate.

The skier below has failed to turn around the marker and winds up wide of the inside pole of the gate. It is a common failing of novice racers. Repeated down the hill, on every gate, it would result in a line of descent far greater than Steve's, shown in the (first) sequence. A greater distance traveled down a slalom can add up to whole seconds of time before the skier reaches the finish line.

Short Giant Slalom Turns

Shorter, faster turns are created when the inside poles of each open gate are set closer to the fall line down the hill. Here a giant slalom course has been set which no longer requires the skier to move so much back and forth across the hill.

   With shorter turns, tactics change. The skier should no longer aim his skis at the outside pole of the gate, but rather at the inside third of the opening in the gate.

The marker again has been planted in the snow, vertically above the inside pole of the gate, to indicate where the skier should turn.

Note how his line of descent is now well inside the track left in the snow from the previous turns done through wide-set, long-turn giant slalom gates on pages 268-69. In the sequence above, Steve's skis move less across the fall line; his upper body is aimed downhill.

Short Slalom Turns

Here single-pole slalom gates have been set with the inside poles closer to the fall line, and then totally in the fall line in the photo on page 284.

The first setting, at right, consists of open gates. Steve aims his skis at an area just inside the pole and uses the helper marker to turn. Note that his skis move very little in and out of the fall line.

The extreme form of short-turn slalom consists of gates set so

that the inside poles line up with the fall line. Above, Phil skis through open gates. At right, the gates are closed and set vertically down the hill in a flush. Helper poles stuck in the snow force the skier to turn close to the pole, with almost no directional change across the hill.

Short-Turn Errors

Here and on the next page are examples of what can go wrong in short-turn giant slalom and slalom should the skier ignore rules to find the correct line.

In the short-turn giant slalom, note that his skis are aimed at the outside (unseen) pole of the gate, not at the inside third of the opening in the gate as they should be. As a result he turns outside the marker, traveling a far greater distance than is efficient. Much of his problem stems from an absence of up-and-down motion. He fails to pressure the front of the ski and, with the consequent lack of definitive edging or carving, his skis skid around, making it impossible to follow a precise line down the hill.

The skier in the flush [*opposite page*] fails to aim his skis downhill. Turning wide and skidding on each pole not only slows his speed but causes him to drop lower and lower on each turn; this is called "getting behind." By the time he reaches the last gate in the flush, he will be unable to make it around the pole.

In a flush the same rule applies for short turns: keep the skis aimed at an area close to the inside pole—or, in the case of a closed gate, the upper pole—of the gate. In the flush [*below*], note that Phil's skis barely move out of the fall line.

Long to Short Turns

Many kinds of terrain and trails call for the skier to go from long turns to a series of short turns, such as when a trail changes from wide to narrow.

Slalom and giant slalom courses are really a series of challenges to the racer to go from long turns to short turns, and back to long turns. Such "rhythm changes," as they are called, are challenges built into races by course-setters.

The racer will meet the challenge successfully if he or she keeps in mind the rules for line described earlier in this section. In a long turn aim the skis at the outside pole of the oncoming gate; in a short turn aim at an area in the gate opening close to the inside pole.

The main difference in going from long to short turns is to anticipate the change before it happens.

On pages 291 and 292, a series of widely set, long-turn open gates in a slalom suddenly changes to a flush. On the facing page, Steve anticipates the change while he is still in the long-turn gates. In fact he treats the final wide-set open gate as if its inside pole were part of the oncoming flush. Instead of directing his skis at the outside pole of the last open gate, he aims at the area near the inside pole. The result is to aim his skis downhill at the flush. If he had not directed his skis in this way, Steve would have come sideways at the top pole of the flush, as the skier has done on page 292, losing speed and very likely getting behind.

Long to short turns, incorrect

Short to Long Turns

The same rule that applies for long to short turns works, in reverse, when the gate combinations make it necessary to go from short to long turns. The skier must anticipate the oncoming change and work on a new line of attack before arriving at the wider set gates.

Here Phil solves the problem in the last gate of the flush. He aims his skis across the hill at the outside pole of the first long-turn open gate.

Before he reaches the first open gate Phil already has established the rhythm and line of long-turn skiing.

Sum-Up

The purpose of this section has been to show that skiing—like tennis or basketball—is a game of tactics as well as mechanical skills.

We learn the skills of skiing by mastering the mechanics of the turn. The more miles of skiing we experience, the more the skills of turning and sliding become automatic, absorbed into our muscle memory.

With the underlying skills we can then proceed to concentrate on where and when to turn, how to use terrain, how to find the fastest line down a slalom or NASTAR course.

Finally, by knowing the tactics of skiing, we can begin to think about applying our skills to different situations. We are ready to marry technique to tactics.

SEVEN

STRUGGLE FOR THE WORLD CUP

It's the popular view in the hyped, television-happy world of sports that the ultimate achievement of an athlete is winning an Olympic gold medal. In the expert's view of ski racing, however, the top competitor is the one who wins the World Cup.

Unlike an Olympic gold medal, which an athlete wins for performance in a single race, the World Cup is awarded to the racers—one man and one woman—who amass the most points in a winter-long series of races, from early December to late March, in as many as ten different countries. Racers, coaches, ski journalists, and knowledgeable fans are unanimous in agreeing that the winner of the World Cup is the best skier of the year. Rosi Mittermaier—who came within 12/100ths of a second of being the only woman in ski racing history to win three gold medals in a single Olympics—said at Innsbruck that winning the World Cup was still more important.

The idea of the World Cup was conceived in 1966 by the European ski writer Serge Lang. Until that time international ski competition had consisted of the biennial Olympics and World Championships and a few annual classics like the Hahnenkamm at Kitzbühel, the Lauberhorn at Wengen, and the Arlberg Kandahar. The racers seldom came to the United States.

Serge's idea was to schedule a series of races in which competitors would accumulate points as the season progressed. The schedule would include races in the States.

While still a journalist writing for a number of European papers, Serge became the source of energy for the new tour and its principal organizer.

Serge is a strong personality and, occasionally, can aggravate people. But we've enjoyed him, and even our controversies have been fun. We didn't see eye to eye with him on the introduction of the Super G race into the World Cup and we refused to compete in it. That was hard for him to take. But we continued to respect each other. Serge understands the press and he knows how to sell the World Cup.

Serge's interest in the World Cup is so powerful that it colors all his reporting. After Phil became a contender for the World Cup, Serge inevitably was waiting to interview him at the finish line.

"Serge rarely talked to me but he would always talk to Phil," recalls Steve, "because Phil was leading in the World Cup and I didn't stand a chance. The outcome of the World Cup was all that mattered to Serge. Even if I won a race, rather than interview me Serge would go over to *Phil* and ask him, 'How do you feel about being beaten by your brother?' "

In the early days of the World Cup, before our time, no one questioned the concept of an all-round competition, since there were guys then like Killy and Schranz who competed regularly in all three Alpine events. And there were fewer races those first years, so the competitors had time to train in all three disciplines.

In the 1970s, however, ski racing became more and more specialized. Downhill, particularly, became almost a distinct sport, with separate coaches and training programs, athletes who skied downhill only, special skis, wind-tunnel experiments, and special suits and fabrics to cut wind resistance.

By 1978 the specialization got so pronounced that almost no one was competing in major meets except as either a downhill specialist or a gate skier. In the Arlberg Kandahar—which for years had traditionally had a combined result—Bob McKee, a good recrea-

The Boss: Serge Lang,
creator of the World Cup.

DICK NEEDHAM

tional skier from Stowe, Vermont, who managed to enroll himself as a member of the Irish Ski Team, won third place in the A-K combined. With so few racers going for combined results, McKee showed that a competent male skier could come out of the base lodge in 1978 and win one of the classic medals in ski racing.

Meanwhile, for political reasons, the FIS kept adding countries, and more and more races, to the World Cup tour. The racers found less and less time to train for each increasingly specialized discipline.

Instead of reducing the number of races, as they should have done, the World Cup organizers, led by Serge, kept toying around with the point formula. They thought by changing the way points were handed out, it would give the racers incentives to compete in all three events. But they were doing this at a time when ski manufacturers were handing out more and more money for results in individual races. The racers naturally went where the money was, and all-round competition took a back seat.

It was especially frustrating to see Ingemar Stenmark win three overall World Cups in a row without once competing in downhill. To prevent this from happening again, the FIS introduced combined points in the 1978–79 World Cup. Henceforth, a racer could earn bonus points based on his linked results in a downhill and slalom, or a downhill and a giant slalom.

The result was again something of an outrage when Peter Luescher, a Swiss racer, won the World Cup while placing first in only one ski race over the entire winter. Almost as bad was Phil coming in third after missing the whole tail end of the season due to his broken ankle.

The following winter of 1980 the rules were again revised, this time to allow a racer to count his five best race results toward the World Cup instead of only three. That seemed to work better. Andy and Hanni Wenzel did a brother-sister act, winning the men's and women's World Cups, and this time everyone was happy with the outcome. Andy scored good points in all three Alpine disciplines and enjoyed the best season of his career. He beat Stenmark by four

Andy Wenzel won the World Cup in 1980 and proved that the new point formula worked. Sister Hanni captured the women's trophy and hammered home the point. Phil is at right.   HUBERT SCHRIEBL

points to win the cup, and of his 204-point total, 65 came in the combined, while Stenmark had no combined points because he still refused to race in downhill events.

The next winter Andy changed boots and proceeded to experience a lot of trouble. In our opinion a racer shouldn't make a major equipment change in mid-career. We've found it hard enough to change models within one manufacturer's line, let alone switch to another ski company. Andy went back to his old boots a couple of years later and made a comeback. Andy never gives up. He's a real competitor, and one of the nicest guys on the whole tour.

Phil won in 1981 by six points over Ingemar, with more than a quarter of his points derived from combined results, and with Ingemar finally managing to earn some combined points himself. He did it by entering the only World Cup downhill he ever raced in.

Oddly enough, Ingemar chose the toughest trail in the world to make what was both his debut and his final downhill appearance. It was in the Hahnenkamm at Kitzbühel. He cruised down the course and came in eleven seconds behind the winning time, placing thirty-fourth. Phil came in ninth.

Because so few of the World Cup racers were in the competition for combined points, Stenmark's downhill result was enough to give him fifteen combined points. Normally a quiet guy, he was so elated by the result that he jumped over a snow fence into the arms of his girlfriend, a Lufthansa stewardess whose existence up to then was unknown to the press. The next day the European papers headlined that Stenmark had discovered love and the downhill all in the same day.

It also says something about the development of downhill racing as a specialized sport that Stenmark's time on the Hahnenkamm downhill was not far off Jean-Claude Killy's winning time more than a dozen years before.

For Phil the strategy for winning the World Cup had been clear from the start. "I determined to enter all the downhill races early in the season that were linked to slalom or giant slalom results and would, therefore, give me combined points. As soon as I could win the maximum of seventy-five combined points, I could stop racing downhill and concentrate on slalom and giant slalom—both to get more points and to deny Stenmark points.

"The problem—and it illustrates the difficulty a racer experiences in trying to ski all three Alpine events—was that I was unable to complete my goal of winning seventy-five combined points until early in February. I had to enter downhill after downhill. As a result, my slalom and giant slalom scores suffered—I finished no better than fourth. After I reached my goal of seventy-five combined points, though, I was finished with the downhills, and I was able to win three races over Stenmark and gain eighty-eight World Cup points. Not having to train for downhill allowed me to refocus on the events in which I do best.

"Meanwhile, of course, Stenmark was trying to prevent me from making points, which is part of the strategy of winning the World Cup. In the cup's complicated scoring, a racer is limited to a 125-point maximum in each discipline. That winter Ingemar had maxed out in giant slalom, having won a half-dozen races, each worth twenty-five points. He couldn't win any more points.

"On the other hand, if I came in third or better at Laax, Switzerland, the final competition, I could pick up enough World Cup points to overtake Ingemar in the season's standings. Any result worth fifteen points or more would replace a fifth-place giant slalom result worth eleven points I had earned earlier in the season. A second place worth twenty points, or a third worth fifteen, would do the job.

"Still, if Stenmark and another racer could come in one-two at Laax, that would deny me the second place I needed to win the World Cup.

"That very nearly happened. In the second run I started just behind the Russian Aleksandr Zhirov and just ahead of Stenmark. At the finish my time wasn't fast enough to catch Zhirov's time for both runs, so it all rested on what Ingemar would do.

"He skied the course well, but his second run time was considerably slower than his first. The two together put him just behind me in third place. It was that close for the first World Cup ever won by an American."

Finally, Phil had figured a way to beat the Swede, who discovered love and the downhill on the same day.

RUSSELL/KELLY

The win at Laax was Zhirov's fourth in a row. That winter the Russians had become rising stars on the World Cup circuit, and there were rumors that the Soviets had a master plan to dominate ski racing.

The ascendency of the Russian star was brief, however. The next season they did far less well, and during the summer of 1982, Zhirov was killed in an auto accident. At the Sarajevo Olympics no Russian men skiers even came to the Alpine events.

What happened?

We believe the Russians simply overtrained. At one point their regimen had them on skis 150 days out of season, and that didn't include race days and winter training! (If we skied even as many as 150 days a year we thought it was too much.)

The Russians may have been trying to emulate their successes in sports like weight lifting, and if that was their aim it was misdirected. In lifting weights, as in other indoor sports, you train every day in the same room. The conditions don't change. But to ski as many days as the Russians did meant that they were on summer snow a lot—glacier ice or old, salted snow. It's not the same. It requires a different technique. So it's very likely that when they came back to natural winter conditions, they found they had lost their feel for the snow. They also had to change their equipment.

A huge amount of training may be needed when a racer is coming up, but when you're in peak form—as the Russians were in 1981—it can hurt you. And so the Russian rocket sputtered out. They are hardly seen on the circuit anymore, for if the Russians know they don't have winning athletes, they tend not to want to compete.

It continues to trouble the World Cup that not enough competitors are trying to win the overall trophy. One improvement would be to allow any skier in the top thirty in slalom or giant slalom to ski in downhill. Then, rather than award points in the regular way to the top fifteen finishers in the combined, they could award points to racers based on their percentage of the winning downhill time.

Let's say, for example, that a slalomer is twenty seconds behind the winner in a downhill. He would not be allowed to earn combined points. But if he were ten seconds out in a 100-second downhill, he would be awarded points. It's an idea worth trying.

The FIS should be commended for trying to keep alive the goal of a racer being a three-event skier. It's a pity they get so little help from the coaches, especially the Austrians, who are notorious specialists and don't seem to have any interest at all in the aims of the World Cup.

On the other hand, the introduction of special combined races at the World Championships was a Mickey Mouse idea. Since every country has a chance, if it wishes, to enter racers in the tougher downhill, slalom, and giant slalom events at the World Championships, why create lesser events for a separate combined? The old paper-combined was a truer rating of the best all-round skier compared with an event that combines just downhill, on a shortened course, and slalom. The top racers laugh at it.

In 1982 the new World Championship combined was won by Michel Vion, who was thirty-fifth in the World Cup, winning only ten World Cup race points that winter. Even Vion was quoted as saying of the special combined, *"C'est ridicule."*

The rule changes and new events introduced by the FIS are a puzzlement. The FIS consists of a bunch of older men—many of them former competitors from days when ski racing was quite different—who aren't in very close touch with today's racers. Marc Holder, the president, who is Swiss, has tried sporadically to meet with the racers on the World Cup and discuss their needs. But then the racers can't agree among themselves, with the downhillers having desires quite different from the technical skiers. So the racers don't present a single viewpoint that the FIS can work from.

We were opposed to the FIS's introduction of the Super G race in the World Cup. Knowing that an excessive number of races is already a problem with the World Cup, especially given the lack of time to train for three disciplines—let alone four—you have to ask why they introduced such an event.

The idea of the Super G was to create a race which both downhillers and giant slalom skiers might have an equal chance to win. It is supposed to be a high-speed g.s. or a low-speed downhill, however you choose to look at it. To us, it looks like a butchered ski race. So they threw in a few bumps on the Super G courses to add television excitement, as if we needed more accidents and spills in ski racing for the benefit of the competitors.

Serge Lang pressured us to compete in the Super G, but we refused. When Phil was lagging in the 1983 World Cup, "Serge needled me, saying, 'Now maybe you'll change your mind about the Super G.'

"I replied, 'Serge, you're going to screw up the sport.'

" 'But what if you lose the World Cup by fifteen points?'

" 'The Super G is bad for ski racing, and ski racing is more important than the World Cup. It wouldn't bother me at all—now leave me alone!' I was pissed."

One reason the Super G was invented was because the press had declared the two-run giant slalom boring. They said the first run was like watching grass grow, because the only thing that counted was how the second run came out.

Well, that just shows a lack of appreciation of ski racing. The thing about slalom and g.s. is that the racer has two chances. If he has a bad run, or makes mistakes in one run—and then puts together a second run that is awesome, completely flawless—he can still win the race. It's exciting to see a racer pull out all the stops and attack the course. We'd see less of that in giant slalom if we went back to a single run, as in the Super G.

The only ski race that is truly exciting for the general TV viewer to watch is the side-by-side parallel. There, you can see two people on the screen at once, you can tell who is winning. On the other hand, in the World Cup and the Olympics, you see only one guy on the course at a time. An electronic display flashes his time. Only after the first dozen starters have crossed the finish do you learn the outcome. Before that you can't tell who's winning, or why.

Parallel races are fun. There is one at the end of each World Cup season that doesn't usually count for points, but the top thirty-two racers in the World Cup who are still there enter it nevertheless.

The night before the 1978 parallel at Arosa, in Switzerland, there was a big party for the racers. At two in the morning we rode home in a van with Ingemar Stenmark. We had to be up at seven in the morning to race, so we didn't have a lot of sleep. And with Ingemar already having wrapped up the World Cup, the race didn't count for anything.

The parallel is run in heats, like a tennis ladder. There are sixteen pairs of racers. Each pair of racers takes two runs, switching courses for the second run. The winner goes on to the next heat. In the end two finalists compete in the last two runs. Phil made it to the finals.

"It was Ingemar and me, and two courses—one was slow at the bottom, the other was fast. You could never win on the slow course. If you happened to start on the fast course, as Ingemar did, you had to build a substantial lead to carry yourself to victory.

"After the first run I rode up on the T-bar lift with Ingemar. He had beaten me by 52/100ths of a second in the first run. He turned to me and said, 'It's not enough.'

"Ingemar was right, as usual. I wound up beating him by a couple of hundredths of a second. He had just won his third World Cup, and it gave me a big lift to have beaten him."

Parallel course racing isn't as tough as conventional slalom, where it's just yourself and the clock. A lot of the time in parallel races you don't have to do anything because the other guy may have fallen higher on the course, so he's out of it. You just cruise to the finish.

Because a number of downhillers ski in the World Cup final parallel, and because it's essentially two slalom courses set side by side, the slalom racers find it easier to do well. There's luck involved too. If you manage to wind up racing against a number of fallers, you're less tired as you continue than a racer who has to battle in each heat.

Bob Beattie was very successful in introducing parallel-course professional ski racing in the U.S. At one time he recruited big names like Killy, Kidd, and Spider Sabich to race. But then the American pro tour became mostly a retirement ground for World Cup racers in decline, for Europa Cup and B racers who never made it to the top, and retired U.S. Ski Team members.

Head-to-head racing popularized the American pro circuit, but it never caught on internationally.

Bob gave up running the pro tour after the winter of 1981. He was the U.S. Ski Team Alpine director in the 1960s. We know him mostly from the other side of the ABC microphone. He and Frank Gifford do the best job of anyone telecasting skiing. They make the races colorful to the public, although, as racers, we sometimes find Bob's commentary overdone.

Bob probably saw a lot of our videotape, and he might say that one of us was using more hip than the other, or that we were getting the shoulder in too much in the turn. Bill Marolt, on the other hand, talked mostly about pole planting. We used to joke that if pole planting was as important as Marolt made it out to be, they would have called the sport "poling."

Bob Beattie was a former U.S. Ski Team coach, but we knew him only from the other side of the mike. His style of leadership wouldn't have worked for us.

Had Beattie been a coach in the 1980s he would have been at odds with the kids on the team and would have had little success. Our impression of the team in the sixties was that if you didn't do it Beattie's way, you didn't get to do it at all. Today the team training programs are tailored more to individuals.

No question, though, Beattie has done a lot for the sport of skiing in America. He helped Serge Lang start the World Cup, and he brought the races to the United States. He also made a determined effort to promote parallel, dual-course ski racing, and it's still around, even if it hasn't caught on internationally.

The World Cup is a grueling caravan. You move from country to country, often on a twenty-four-hour basis. Austria and Switzerland have the most rabid ski fans—we were better known there than we were in the States.

We especially liked St. Anton in the Vorarlberg region of Austria. We stayed at the Park Hotel. Gunnar Munthe, who owns the Crazy Kangaroo, a restaurant and bar, would arrange for us to play tennis and basketball.

We also liked Kitzbühel, where we stayed in a castle converted

Ski racing in Europe is big, and the racers are national heroes. From country to country the World Cup caravan is awaited by local fans.

into a hotel. The mountain is like Aspen in that the steeper slopes are at the bottom and the easy skiing on top.

At first we didn't like Italy, but then it grew on us. Val Gardena became a favorite place. We stayed at a hotel run by the sister of Alex Giorgi, the Italian racer. She fed us like royalty, and we must have gained five pounds each whenever we went there. Winter after winter, Italy became better and France worse. We came to believe that the French disliked Americans, and eventually we didn't care to race there. We found the people rude and unfriendly. Oddly enough, however, our race results were usually good in France.

We didn't find Switzerland too lively, but Wengen is beautiful. Isolated from automobile traffic, the resort can be reached by train. Its views of the Eiger are stunning.

Contrary to popular impression, the World Cup doesn't attract a lot of hangers-on and groupies. However many women did follow the tour, they more likely were pursuing the guys on the downhill circuit. The downhillers have a sexier mystique than the technical skiers. Maybe it's their reputation for being kind of crazy, while the gate skiers—the slalom and giant slalom racers—tend to be more conservative.

For two seasons, Phil was pursued by a girl from Zurich whom we called "Judith Fox" because of the fur coat she wore. She hung around the hotel where we were staying, and we had to sneak in and out of the lobby to avoid her. Once she stood outside of the U.S. Ski Team van for an hour in the rain waiting for Phil to come out.

Phil was also pursued by a girl we called "the Rabbit Woman." "She first appeared at Park City in Utah. She had her daughter with her and she presented me with a toy rabbit. It was Easter.

"That summer I was working in Yakima installing swimming pools. I came home from work one day and found another stuffed rabbit in my mailbox. By the house I noticed that someone had tied balloons on to my van and pasted Oreo cookies on the windshield in a pattern that said, 'Hi, Phil.'

"Another day she left a loaf of banana bread. It went on like that. You never knew when she would strike.

"One day I found a brand-new deck of playing cards on the doorstep. A note was attached that asked, 'Who holds all the aces?' In October I went to Europe and, not thinking much about it, took the deck of cards with me. We decided to play hearts one night in the hotel and brought out the Rabbit Woman's deck. We played to the last trick, and still an ace hadn't been played. There were none in the pack. Then I recalled her note. Who was holding all the aces? It was the Rabbit Woman!

"Finally in Yakima, where she had evidently moved, she left her phone number. I called her and politely asked her to get lost. I said I was happy with my life and didn't want to get involved. A year later she phoned to apologize."

In the last couple of years we were on the World Cup the crowds noticeably dwindled in size. More and more people are watching the races on television, which makes sense—particularly for downhill and g.s. where TV allows you to see a racer's descent down almost the entire course. Even the press now uses TV monitors at the bottom of the course to follow the action on sections of the course that can't be seen from the finish line.

It's difficult to know what needs to be done to make ski racing more attractive as a spectator sport. Golfers can identify with players they see on television competing on the PGA Tour. They see a pro trying to make a five-foot putt and it could be them. In ski racing, however, the technique and speed of racers are so great that it's hard for viewers to relate.

If more skiers would enter NASTAR they would become ski-racing fans. NASTAR is an easy giant slalom usually set on a hill that is not at all steep. Recreational skiers run the gates just like racers on the World Cup. Having done it a few times, they should find it much easier to appreciate and relate to racing on television. After all, if you hook a ski tip on a pole in NASTAR it isn't really any different from a racer making the same error in a World Cup race. Only the speeds differ.

One reason ski racing lacks interest as a spectator sport is because the outcome of the race is usually known after the first half-dozen racers have finished their second run. In most athletic events, spectator interest is held to the end of the game. But in skiing the best racers start first, and the rest of the field follows.

Ski racing would be popular as a spectator sport in America if more skiers entered NASTAR.   DEL MULKEY

In some World Cup races you have fields of eighty racers, with competitors coming in ten to fifteen seconds out of first place. You can hardly hold public attention with a format like that.

In 1984–85 the FIS ran a couple of slaloms and giant slaloms with the whole field earning FIS points in the first run. The second run was limited to the best thirty finishers starting in the reverse order of their finish in the first run. In this way the best competitors came at the end. Spectators were held in suspense until the final racer descended the course.

The format is interesting, but it depends on the ability of the course preparers to create hard—probably chemically treated—snow that can offer quality skiing to the final racers.

Ski racing is a complex athletic competition in which imperceptible errors often make the difference between winning and losing.

Once Steve won a World Cup race at St. Anton by a fraction of a second, and Andy Wenzel lost it by a tiny mistake. Wenzel was leading after the first run, but we were both right behind him. In his second run Andy was so sure he had won the race that he raised his hands in a victory signal before he reached the finish line. That gesture cost him 2/100ths of a second, enough for Steve to gain the win. With an extra skating step, or a final push to the finish, Wenzel probably would have won.

When a racer loses by a small margin he finds himself asking questions about microscopic details of the runs: "Why didn't I do this instead of that?"

In a final World Cup race at Saalbach, Austria, in 1980, Steve lost to Ingemar Stenmark by 11/100ths of a second after leading in the first run. "Afterwards, I remembered that I had jammed an edge on soft snow eight gates from the finish. It probably caused me to lose speed on the flat.

"Concentration is a key to the chemistry of ski racing. In a World Cup slalom race at Cortina, Italy, Phil and I were in position to come in one-two, with me out in front. Two thirds of the way down the second run I came to a place where the course became flatter. I found myself muttering, 'You'd better start hustling, you're not even trying.' I suddenly skied more aggressively. If I hadn't, Phil would have squeaked by me.

The World Cup works
this way: Ski like hell
and know the arithmetic.

K2 PHOTO

"That added ounce of aggression added up, probably, to a few hundredths of a second, but it was enough to win. I was lucky enough to have caught myself being lazy."

It can be disheartening to lose a race by a hundredth of a second, which, in terms of distance, may be the equivalent of just a few inches. Then there are those strange days when someone so completely dominates a ski race, you're left scratching your head, wondering why.

In a World Cup race at Kitzbühel there was such a day that belonged to Ingemar Stenmark. We placed second and third, but we were 3 and 3.8 seconds behind him. In two runs he completely annihilated us. Why? There was nothing perceptible in his skiing to explain such a large margin of victory.

Maybe we do, after all, need changes in ski racing to make it more visual and easier for the spectator to follow. But whatever those changes are, they'll have to be made through trial and error, not imposed on the sport like the Super G. Meanwhile, by making every race during the winter count, the World Cup has fulfilled its original promise of adding excitement to ski racing.

How the World Cup Works

The World Cup consists of a pair of beautiful crystal trophies awarded annually to the best man and woman skier in international racing as determined in a season-long series of races.

The races start in early December and continue to the end of March, with a break for Christmas and a three-week hiatus in February for the Olympics, World Championships, or national championships of the different countries. Race results in the Olympics and World Championships do not count toward the World Cup.

In each of a couple of dozen downhill, slalom, and giant slalom/ Super G races held over the winter in as many as ten countries, racers can win points. Points are awarded in each race as follows:

Place	World Cup Points	Place	World Cup Points
1st	25	9th	7
2nd	20	10th	6
3rd	15	11th	5
4th	12	12th	4
5th	11	13th	3
6th	10	14th	2
7th	9	15th	1
8th	8		

The point system reflects a high premium placed on a racer finishing in the first three, but it also rewards consistency over the season. If you fall and don't finish a race you get no points, which leaves that many fewer races in which to make points.

A top World Cup racer can win only a maximum of 125 points in any one of the three disciplines. If there are ten giant slalom/ Super G races in a winter, and a racer wins five, he can win more World Cup points only by competing in another Alpine discipline—slalom or downhill.

However, a racer can replace lesser points with better points. Phil won the World Cup in 1981 this way. Going in at the end of the season, he had recorded results in five giant slalom races. But one of them was a fourth place, worth eleven points. By coming in second in the last giant slalom at Laax, he was able to replace his previous fourth-place result with a second place worth twenty points, thus increasing his World Cup total by nine points. On the other hand, Stenmark had already won five giant slalom races worth 125 points and could earn no more. All he could do was to try to beat Phil and deny him second place.

In addition to the overall World Cup there are individual honors given to racers who lead in each of the disciplines. To a downhiller who wins the greatest number of World Cup points in that discipline, and doesn't compete in the other events, the winning of the downhill World Cup is all-important. The slalom and giant slalom World Cups were especially prized by Ingemar Stenmark, but in 1982 they went to Phil, in addition to his winning the overall World Cup.

In an effort to get racers to stop specializing and to compete in all three Alpine disciplines, the World Cup introduced combined points in the 1978–79 season. Combined points really are paper results, computed by combining a downhill race result with a slalom, giant slalom, or Super G result in another race.

The races in which competitors can earn combined results are designated on the World Cup calendar at the beginning of the season. Often a downhill and a gate race at the same resort are combined.

A skier trying for combined results is limited to counting his three best results out of five. A racer can't earn more than seventy-five combined points in a season.

Associated with the World Cup is the Nations Cup, awarded annually to the national ski team whose racers—men and women—amass the greatest number of World Cup points during the season. Austria, France, and Switzerland are the only countries to have won the Nations Cup since it was started, along with the World Cup, in the 1966–67 ski season. Oddly enough, the silver Nations Cup trophy is awarded by *SKI*, an American magazine.

The best the United States has done in the overall Nations Cup is to place third, although the U.S. women's ski team won the highest total of points in women's World Cup skiing in 1982. In that same season, the two of us won 80 percent of the World Cup points garnered by the U.S. men's team.

INTEGRATING TECHNIQUE AND TACTICS

If time allows, a skier should try to expand his or her technique beyond the basic turn. There is actually a repertoire of turns and moves in skiing that a student of the sport can acquire. Each is suitable to a different kind of terrain or situation.

Equipped with a repertoire of turns and traversing actions, the skier can begin to think about how to apply them to different tactical situations.

In Section 5 we studied the tactics of skiing by putting the skier in gates. Gates call for the skier to turn at a specific place on the hill. *When* to turn also calls for tactical decisions.

Different tactics may also suggest different techniques. For example, if tactics call for a skier to cross the hill to reach a wide-set open gate, he may draw from his technique repertoire a laterally

stepped turn, going from the inside edge of the downhill ski to the uphill edge of the uphill ski, followed by a glide, and then the initiation of the turn on the inside edge of the outside ski.

In this section we move into the highest level of skiing—the integration of ski technique with tactics.

Inside-Outside Move in Long Turns

Below is a NASTAR-type course, with the gates set apart to create a series of long turns. The tactic is for Steve to gain a line across the hill that directs his skis at the outside pole of the oncoming gate. In this situation he steps off the inside edge of the downhill ski (outside ski of the previous turn) and onto the outside edge of the uphill ski.

This lateral move allows him to align his skis with the outside pole of the next gate. He steps uphill to gain a new line, glides briefly on the uphill edge of the uphill ski, then directs it onto its inside edge to initiate the new turn around the marker.

Here the technique of the inside edge-outside edge move has been married to a tactic of finding the right line to ski through the gates.

(sequence continued on next page)

Inside-Inside Move

Here the technique of the inside-inside move is integrated with the tactic of having the best line through the gates.

The skier comes out of the top gate finding that his skis are correctly pointed at the outside pole of the next gate. There is no

need to alter line so—to initiate the turn more quickly—he steps immediately onto the inside edge of the uphill ski (the outside ski of the new turn) and turns around the marker flag.

On the final pole he is in the completion phase of the turn and prepares to step onto the outside (uphill) edge of the uphill ski to correct his line to the next gate.

Inside Move in Long-Turn Slalom

At right and continuing on page 326, Phil is photographed in a setting of open slalom gates that creates a series of across-the-hill turns. He is skiing on a training course at White Pass. Everything looks very simple, but the action is so fast and furious here that the eye—and the camera—don't catch quite all of it.

"Notice that my skis, coming out of an earlier gate, are aimed across the hill at the outside pole of the gate through which I'll turn. I lean my body toward the oncoming turn, point the outside [uphill] ski in the path of the new turn it will carve. This was done with a rapid step off the downhill ski, creating a momentary wedge shape of the skis. Ha! You thought the old stem was dead? Well, it seems to have been born again here.

"In fact, what I've done is to move very fast onto the inside edge of the new turning ski—so fast that I quickly come across the fall line and zap the inside pole of the gate. It is what I call my real inside move.

(sequence continued on next page)

"There is absolutely no step here onto an uphill ski still aiming across the hill. Rather, the step is onto a ski that I've already pointed into the turn. This is a much faster move in skiing than a lateral step and turn. Repeated in the right places, several times on a course, it means whole fractions of seconds cut from the racer's time."

The nature of the gate setting—a tactical situation—allowed Phil to apply a specific technique to save time.

Inside-Outside Move, Short G.S.

Here is a different marriage of technique and tactics. Steve is moving at high speed down a combination of giant slalom gates creating a series of short, fall-line turns.

The speed of his skiing gives him an aggressive opportunity to extract energy from his skis and propel himself faster down the course. He does it with brief skate steps.

The force of his first turn stores energy in the tails of the skis. He unleashes it with a quick stepping motion onto the edged uphill ski. He has moved from the inside edge of the downhill ski in the completion phase of the turn onto the outside edge of what will be the steering ski in the next turn.

In a split second he moves the unweighted skis into the fall line, aiming them at the area next to the inside pole of the gate. He steers the turn on the outside ski. The force of the turn in its completion phase stores new energy in the skis to launch him into the next turn.

Although meeting the tactical challenges of skiing through the gates can bring out the best in technique, it can also bring out the worst in a less-experienced skier, as seen below. Concentrating on tactics, the skier suddenly seems to forget everything he learned in ski school. The most common error in gate skiing among recreational skiers is bending at the waist. The skier feels secure in bending over the front of his skis, but his body actually is frozen in a rigid stance. It is difficult for him to pivot the skis in a new direction because his body cannot move up and down and the skis are stuck on the snow, weighted so that they want to keep turning. Note on the opposite page how Steve, in the same kind of turn, angulates to pressure the outside ski and avoids waist-bending.

White Pass Turn, Short G.S.

Here Steve opts for quickness in an adaptation of a certain technique to tactics.

Coming out of a short turn in the top gate, he decides not to use time or distance in a wide-step move. Rather, he moves quickly onto the inside ski that he has just used in the completion phase of the previous turn. He rolls it on its outside, or downhill, edge and heads directly at the area next to the inside pole of the second gate.

Finally, he picks up the steering phase of the turn on the inside edge of the turning ski, and gains a fraction of a second in the process.

Note the result of using the White Pass Turn, a technique, in achieving a superior tactic.

Positioning the Turn

Here we have isolated frames from a photo sequence to indicate the importance in modern ski racing of making the turn at the right time and the right place. Notice how Steve's turn is mostly completed before he reaches the inside pole of the top gate. But also notice how his eyes are aimed ahead at the next gate. The positioning of his turn has been determined by the positioning of the next gate, which he anticipates by looking ahead.

The old rule in racing, you'll remember, was to turn high on an open gate to be ready for the next gate. But the simple rule of turning high on a gate can lead to the error of double turning. Coming out of the gate on too high a line can actually force the skier to make a second correcting turn.

On the other hand, failure to turn properly around the inside pole of the gate can lead the racer on too straight a line down the hill. He would end on too low a line and have to fight to go uphill to make the next gate.

EIGHT

ALL THE WAY
TO THE BANK

Ski racing has come a long way from the days when Austria's Karl Schranz was thrown out of the 1972 Winter Olympics for thumbing his nose at Avery Brundage by making money from an "amateur" sport.

Today's World Cup operates much like any other professional sports tour except that most of its athletes also compete in the Olympics. The racers at the very top are hard-nosed guys. Substantial dollars, marks, and francs ride on the outcome of every race.

Outsiders tend to think of the World Cup as a glamorous grand tour of amateur athletes jetting from country to country, with beautiful women in tow, expensive restaurants, and celebrities hanging on. In truth it's a moving caravan of tough professional racers, ski mechanics, and ink-stained sportswriters. The racers take their careers seriously.

This chapter tells in print, for the first time, how a top racer makes money in the big leagues of World Cup skiing. Since manufacturers pay money for results, and Phil had the best results, it's his story to tell.

At the time I began winning international ski races, important changes were going on in the rules of the sport.

As a result of Karl Schranz's ejection from the '72 Winter Games at Sapporo by the International Olympic Committee, and of other incidents involving under-the-table payments to top racers, the FIS took the lead in the early 1970s to make IOC policy more realistic in dealing with the finances of athletes. Eligibility to compete in the Olympics was liberalized.

The most important reform was to allow an international sports federation, such as the FIS, to pretty much write its own rules governing payments to athletes and how they could be made. In effect the IOC was saying that it wanted to wash its hands of the responsibility for making judgments about individual athletes. Let the separate sports-governing bodies deal with the problems of their own competitors.

The FIS responded by allowing ski racers to receive money from equipment manufacturers as long as the money was channeled through the athlete's national ski federation.

For the first time manufacturers of skis, boots, bindings, poles, and goggles could promote their products openly using the pictures of ski racers and rewarding the racers openly by making payments to them through checks sent via their national ski federations. Previously, companies had been slipping money under the table so as not to cause a racer to lose his amateur eligibility.

When I first joined the U.S. Ski Team affairs hadn't progressed quite this far, but we were allowed to receive what were called "broken time payments."

In theory, broken time payments were to compensate a racer for lost income while he was competing. In reality it was something different.

Since it was hard to find a job for the three or four months a year you weren't competing, and since all expenses were covered while you were competing, broken time payments—approved by the Olympic Committee—were used to keep a racer going while he *wasn't* skiing.

The funds to make the broken time payments came from a pool of ski equipment suppliers who paid for the right to have their products used by the U.S. Ski Team.

It wasn't much. In the course of a year of training and racing with the B team, for example, I was given $2,400 to stay alive. It was no big deal. You sure couldn't go out and build a house with it.

Fortunately, in the nine months when I did compete, all my bills were picked up by the ski team. Broken time payments got me through the other three months.

With the coming of the new rules of amateurism, the sport—or business, as it partly became—of ski racing underwent a financial transformation. Companies seeking to promote their products through the image of racing began to buy athletes.

"If you ski on our product, we'll pay you so much money," they said.

But first they still had to join the official supplier pools of the different national ski teams. And then the companies had to have skis or boots good enough for a racer to win on.

If a ski doesn't perform well, in the long run it doesn't really matter how much money a company offers the racer because ultimately the racer won't win. Steve and I have known racers whose careers virtually went down the tubes because they took the money to get on the wrong skis. In turn, without race victories, the companies themselves can't run advertisements in the ski magazines headlining how so-and-so won on their skis. So there has to be product integrity. The ski has to be made well enough to win on.

These changes coincided with the arrival of Hank Tauber as Alpine program director of the U.S. Ski Team.

We were just nineteen years old when Hank put together the first contracts we negotiated with ski equipment manufacturers. Steven and I signed them. They were four-year deals with the very same companies we work for today: K2 Skis, Lange boots, Smith goggles, and Marker bindings.

We received 100 percent of the money for the ski hardware we used; in effect, checks were sent by the companies to the ski team, then the team turned around and paid the money to us. On the other hand, payments made by apparel and other companies whose products benefitted the team as a whole largely did not get to us. For example, since all the racers wore a team uniform supplied by

An Olympic medal
(with two FIS medals):
Worth more than its
weight in gold.

Descente, that company's rights money was kept by the team. By the same token we weren't free to sign contracts with automobile manufacturers or soft-drink companies who wanted product ruboff from ski racing. Subaru, for example, has been the team's biggest backer, but the company's ads play up the use of the car by the ski team as a whole.

Basically, the money I could receive through the ski team came from skis, boots, bindings, poles, and goggles. With Hank's help in 1976, we negotiated four-year deals.

If we had wanted, we could have signed just one-year contracts. I felt we could make more by negotiating long-term deals. The companies, after all, weren't about to dish out a lot of money if there was a chance of your switching products the next winter. Or if they did pay more money short-term to get you to switch products, you'd never have enough time to learn to ski well with their ski or boot. Your results in competition would suffer.

From the beginning my contracts—like those of the top European racers—had victory schedules.

For example, my first contract with K2 Skis—good to 1980—paid me a base of $15,000 a year. If I won a World Cup race, which I had not yet done when the contract was made, I would make an additional $5,000. Second place was worth $3,000, third place $1,500. The payments were scaled down to fifth place.

Those were payments just for the ski. I also had a victory payments schedule from Lange boots and for the other products. Conceivably, I could win as much as $10,000 in a single World Cup race. And there were as many as twenty slalom and giant slalom races in which I would be competing each winter.

Individual race victories weren't the only way I could make money. If I won one of the individual World Cup titles for my season-long performance in slalom or giant slalom, there would be an additional payment. An individual title was worth $10,000 for first place, less for second and third. And winning the overall World Cup title would have been worth $20,000 for the title itself, with scaled payments for second and third in the final standings.

If I did nothing at all I would still make the $15,000 base just for racing on the ski.

The best thing about my K2 contract, however, was that year by year the previous season's winnings for my standings in the World Cup overall and individual titles created a new higher base compensation for the following season. For example, if I started the 1977–78 season with a base of $20,000 and wound up making $25,000 from my World Cup standings, my new base, starting out the 1978–79 season, would be $45,000.

It was Hank Tauber who put the year-to-year escalator agreement together with K2, and it worked out something fierce. By the time I reached the last year of the original four-year agreement, 1980, it was worth $80,000 just to ski on the product.

I had no such escalator, at least initially, in my Lange boot and Marker binding contracts, in which I was paid the same base over the four years, plus victory winnings.

In addition to the World Cup victory schedule, I could make money for medals won in the Olympic and World Ski Championship races held every two years. For skis alone a gold medal was worth $10,000, a silver $5,000, and a bronze $2,500. A National Championships win in the U.S. had a $1,000 price tag.

It all added up. For a kid who didn't have two nickels to rub together in 1972, and for many winters couldn't afford the transportation to get to some races, I was salting away big dollars.

After the Olympic season of 1980 I was ready to negotiate new contracts for the next four years. April to April, they would carry me through the 1984 winter, including the Sarajevo Olympics.

For the 1980–84 period Marker switched to the escalator system. I started with a base of $20,000 going to the end of the 1981 season, then escalated to a new base the next season, depending on my World Cup standings. By 1984 my Marker base alone—exclusive of individual race victories—was worth $80,000 a year.

Under the new four-year agreement Lange paid me $20,000 a year in base, plus wins.

My deal with K2 also changed. Under the previous contract my base had kept going up, but now, in place of the escalator clause, K2 agreed to pay me a flat $100,000 a year to 1984, plus victory payments.

At the time I thought it was a smart move. A racer never knows if he's going to have a good year or a bad year, and I was guaranteeing myself at least $400,000 in income. If I were injured and couldn't race, I would still be paid, as I would with the other contracts. On the other hand, if I quit, or didn't race, the companies were not obliged to pay me. I had to stay active.

Looking back, the change in the K2 arrangement obviously didn't make me as much money as I would have made had I retained the escalator. I won three World Cups during those four years, three individual titles and other high placements, so had I stuck with the escalator, my base from K2 by 1984 could have been $200,000 a year. It would have skyrocketed.

Nevertheless, I'm satisfied. Both K2 and I got a fair shake. The ski company paid a hell of a lot of money, though not as much as if they had stuck with the old deal. And I felt I was paid well.

In addition to the higher base payments, my new contracts for 1980–84 doubled my payments for winning and placing in individual races. The new victory schedule for using K2 skis and poles gave me $10,000 for winning a World Cup race, compared to the old payment of $5,000. Everything doubled.

Combining all my contracts for skis, boots, bindings, and goggles, a single World Cup win represented a $20,000 payoff. Between 1980 and 1984, I won eleven World Cup races and had so many second places I hate to think about them, each worth half as much as a first place.

Every June the victory payment checks would come in. Including the base payments, I made about $250,000 in 1981. In 1982—the second time I won the World Cup—I made about $400,000, having won not only the overall cup, but also the individual World Cup titles in the slalom, giant slalom, and combined, along with five individual wins and nine second places. It was a bonanza at the bank. Heyday!

In 1983 I actually topped my earnings of the previous season, mainly because my base fee from Marker had jumped way up. I won the overall World Cup and the giant slalom and combined titles.

As things were working out, I had the chance to make as much as half a million dollars in a good competitive year. And it was all aboveboard; the system had been devised and approved by the FIS under the eyes of the International Olympic Committee.

Of course winning races wasn't all we had to do to earn our keep with the ski companies. At the end of each winter we would work with K2 in designing and testing new models of skis for the market. Over the years, too, we made many of personal appearances in ski shops and at industry functions and fund-raisers that benefited not only the manufacturers we were representing but also the ski team.

The contracts obliged me to make appearances, and life hasn't changed much since I retired. Steve and I still turn up at dozens of functions a year—sometimes together, sometimes separately. Our agent books us.

Often I would spend five or six days in a row on the promotion circuit, shaking hands, munching canapés, talking about life on the World Cup and the need to support the ski team. I made no money from the ski team appearances, but without them and the money raised at them, the team would have been in bad shape.

Some ski equipment companies feel they can exist without buying athlete endorsements, though even they will try to market their products by establishing some kind of racing image.

For some companies—like Marker—the main thrust of a product's advertising is to establish its credibility through use by top competitors. This impresses ski retailers as much as, or more than, their customers, and in the ski industry getting the retailer to sell your product is the name of the game. In Europe the racing success of a product carries even greater importance. When a racer like Franz Klammer switches from one manufacturer's skis to another's, the news makes headlines in the Austrian papers.

Under the written—or maybe they're unwritten—rules, a ski equipment manufacturer can use a racer's name and photo in an advertisement, but can't use the sort of outright endorsement I make now that I've turned professional.

A fine line separates what a manufacturer may do in his advertising from what he can't do. It was okay for K2 to say, for example, that Phil Mahre won a race or a medal on their skis, but not okay to say that I go out and win races because I'm on K2s. *SKI* magazine wanted me to work for them when I was racing, but it would have implied an endorsement of the magazine, so I didn't do it, although I work for them now.

While many of the rules were unclear, there was one that wasn't: products from which you made money couldn't be nonski products. That's where the ski team made its money—or most of it.

A kiss to the provider, and new contracts worth a half million a year.

Toward the end of our careers the team created a formula for how much A and B team members received for skiing and acting in TV commercials and print ads, whether shot on the hill or in a studio. When I did a commercial for Canon Camera, for example, I received 10 percent of the rights money while 90 percent went to the ski team. Ten percent isn't a lot, and under the rules what there is of it is assigned to a trust account in the athlete's name. The money doesn't become available to the racer until retirement. It's a good system. The money that's made goes into a trust fund which can be used later when the financial support of the team is gone and the retired racer is trying to make the transition to a new career.

The whole reason to be on the ski team, however, should be to perform, not to make money. Now there's a generation of skiers growing up who believe they should be paid for their services. They think the system should work so that they get 90 percent of the money and the team only 10 percent. If that happened only those few athletes in demand by advertisers would get paid. And the team would get blown away financially.

Cutting the money the other way would result in a whole new game for the racers. The team would have to say to them, "Okay, you want the money, you pay for the coaches, you make and pay for your own plane and hotel reservations—do everything on your own. That's it, and we'll see you in Val d'Isère, France, on December 1!"

It would certainly give the racers a new perspective on life. As things stand now they simply sit back and have things done for them. But under a scheme where the athletes took most of the endorsement money, the team would no longer be able to supply those services.

The ski team faces a basic problem: it's difficult to market the team as a team as long as commercial firms want to market a few individual athletes. I'm sure there were instances when companies wanted ski team endorsements, but only if they could use the Mahres in their ads. If we weren't available, they weren't interested.

In those circumstances it might have been easy for us to say, "Instead of paying the ski team, why not pay us?" But the money had to go to the team, and so it should. The athletes can't exist outside a team structure, not in the Olympics and World Championships, and not even on the World Cup circuit when you consider the logistics of travel and training. Who's going to pay for it?

I think it's okay to have something like the new athletes' rights group on the ski team looking out for the athletes' general interests, but they aren't going to change anything on this basic question. If the racers take a stand and insist on getting all the money, and are prepared to go on strike for it, then there'll be a lockout by their employer, the ski team. It would be like Continental Airlines.

The rights-conscious racers have to remember that they're there not to make money but to compete. If they compete well they'll find plenty of financial rewards, and if they don't succeed competitively at first, it's important to have a financially sound ski team around to take care of them and give them the opportunity to continue to compete and, one day, win.

For a short period there was a way for a World Cup racer to get all the money—by taking out a so-called B License. But only a few racers took advantage of it, and it had a price of its own.

While I made close to half a million my last year on the circuits, I'd say that Ingemar Stenmark must be pulling down a million dollars a year. I probably made as much as Stenmark on ski equipment, but he chose to take out a B License, which meant that he could keep practically all of the endorsement money paid by manufacturers of products, not just ski equipment. To use the example of the Canon camera commercial, Stenmark would keep all of the money—he would pay only the Swedish Ski Federation for training expenses. To bring that about, all he had to do was surrender his right to compete in the Olympics.

Apart from Stenmark, I probably made more money than any other racer on the tour. Certainly there weren't more than half a dozen racers on the whole World Cup circuit making as much as Steve and I, and they would largely be the downhillers like Klammer and Harti Weirather, of Austria, and Steve Podborski, the Canadian. Downhill is called "the king" of ski racing in Europe; it draws the biggest crowds and the most TV and press coverage, and consequently it's the biggest magnet for money.

Canada's Podborski was an easygoing guy, a floater. He was different from Kenny Read, another Canadian downhill star. In 1980 Kenny was irked because Leonard Stock had moved ahead of him in FIS points by winning the Olympic gold medal in downhill at Lake Placid. Kenny stood to lose money on his contract—maybe ten grand—by being ranked behind Stock.

The FIS was lucky that Stenmark and Hanni Wenzel, who each won two gold medals at Lake Placid, were the only racers after the 1980 Olympics to take up B Licenses. You have to wonder how a bunch of supposedly wise old men on the FIS Council could come up with such a bad idea as the B License.

If every racer had decided to take out a B License, there isn't a national ski team federation in the world that would still be afloat. The FIS finally abandoned the B License in 1983 because it was a flop, owing to the fact that the racers still wanted to compete in the Olympics. Perhaps, too, it finally dawned on the FIS that the B License really did have the potential to bankrupt the national ski federations.

While Stenmark clearly benefited financially, taking out a B License proved to be a mistake for Hanni Wenzel. She wasn't that attractive to companies outside of the ski industry, and her race results fell—possibly as a result of her special status on her team. With poor results, you don't attract sponsors.

Even if there had still been a B License in 1984, I wouldn't have taken one. Serge Lang, the organizer of the World Cup, tried to talk us into staying on the circuit. He said the World Cup wouldn't be the same without us competing. Jokingly, I said to him, "Serge, you come up with two million Swiss francs, and we'll stay."

Had he taken us seriously, where would the money have come from? Perhaps he would have tried to persuade the powers-that-be to bend the rules and allow us to do what Stenmark is doing. But in fact we weren't interested in continuing to race on the World Cup, whatever the payoff. I had won three World Cups and an Olympic gold medal. It was time to retire.

I banked a considerable amount of money in my peak years. Thom Weisel, president of the U.S. Ski Team and head of Montgomery Securities in San Francisco, is our financial adviser. He has put me into R&D tax shelters like oil deals and computer chips. He plays the market. With the money from the stock market alone, I could probably live comfortably.

I've brought real estate that over ten years will start to pay off. I have a condominium in Arizona that I rent out and a town house that we live in from time to time because my wife is from Scottsdale. I bought two rentable condos in Yakima and a couple of vacant five-acre lots. One day I may build on them and sell.

Our thoughts about business started in the winter of 1983–84 when Bill Kirschner, the original designer and builder of the K2 ski, and Barry Gordinier, a former K2 marketing man, approached us and asked, "What are you going to do when you're done ski racing?"

Most of the ideas we discussed with the two of them have come to pass. In 1984 we signed new four-year agreements with the same companies whose products we had skied on through our racing careers. We also determined to start a ski apparel business which now is called TWN Corporation.

Although we could have endorsed someone else's skiwear line, after four years what would we have to show for it? So we launched our own line in the hope that someday we'll own a million-dollar company. We also hope to expand our ski training camps to other resorts.

Business challenges me, but I don't find money important. As long as I can live comfortably and give my family a few fringe benefits, I don't need millions. My goal is to maintain a public profile consistent with what I stood for when I was a ski champion.

For sure I don't intend to become a forgotten former racer.

SKIING ICE AND BUMPS, AND OTHER TIPS

One of the reasons we named this book *No Hill Too Fast* is that in addition to reflecting our own love of speed in sports, the title is meant to suggest that people can progress in their skiing if they push harder to ski fast. Conversely, people tend to plateau in technique if they never try to go faster.

A reminder about speed: you need a longer ski to ski fast. Many people plateau in their technique because they stay on a short ski. Speed and ski length go together.

Speed supplies energy to the ski, and if you ski it right, the ski will return that energy to you in your technique. Speed also forces you to improve. Inevitably it brings out errors in your skiing, and eventually you'll crash. But the lessons of falling tend to reinforce learning, as we all know. Progression to steeper hills also is a must.

In skiing today most of the work is done from the waist down. In slalom, in particular, your upper body should be stable and quiet, so that your legs use it as an anchor around which to make the turn.

In long turns, and giant slalom, the skier should stand more square to the skis, rather than to the fall line of the mountain; that is, the upper body tends mostly to be at right angles to the direction

of the skis. But, as we said earlier in this book, there are no rigid body positions in skiing, only movement that projects images of body positions.

The main aim of the skier should be to pressure the turning ski, and angulation is essential to pressuring the outside ski. Angulation—whether accomplished at the hip or at the knee—refers to the action of getting your upper body out and over the ski being turned. That is how you get pressure on it.

Practice your turns lifting the inside ski off the snow. Think of the inside ski as a recovery device, not as a ski used to steer or complete the turn.

One common error of skiers is to remain on their heels. Remember this simple rule, "Shoulders ahead of hips," and you won't go wrong. You should be able to feel the pressure of the boot on your shin at most times.

Skiing Ice

To turn in icy conditions it is essential not to prolong edging, but to make the edge bite quick and sharp.

Uncertain and lacking confidence in skiing on ice, many skiers increase the angle of the edge to the ice and push hard. That is wrong.

The correct way, shown in the sequences on the following pages, is to increase knee angulation and drop the body. Let the force of the turn do the work for you. Make the action of the inside edge of the turning ski very quick and hard. Get onto and off the edge in a split second. The impact, not necessarily a sharper edge angle or holding the edge on the ice, is what will give you edge bite.

Notice in the rearview sequence [*pp. 356-57*] how Steve allows the ski to float over the icy surface. Then, at the precise moment of steering, he increases knee and hip angulation and hits the edge hard. Just as quickly, he gets off the edge and steers toward the new turn with another floating action. There is no skidding, no prolonged dragging of the edges over the ice.

Skiing Ice (continued)

Skiing Ice (continued)

Skiing Bumps

To tell the truth, neither of us is that crazy about skiing moguls, but every now and then we get a bang out of it.

"I like a trail," says Steve, "where maybe a quarter of the run has moguls on it, at most. And if I'm skiing bumps, they might just as well be five feet high. Then I'll go from top to top of the bumps, using a lot of knee absorption.

"Obviously, the less-experienced skier is better off sliding into the troughs between the moguls to steer and complete the turns while using the tops or sides of the bumps to pivot the skis in a new direction.

"As far as instruction? It's more a case of do as I say than do as I do, since I wouldn't advise anyone but a very good skier to go down the bumps the way I do!"

(sequence continued on page 361)

Skiing Bumps (continued)

Pole Planting

Ski racers spend hours of drill on the use of poles because it's so critical to making the turn in the right place when you're skiing through gates.

The timing of the pole plant is less critical in uncrowded, free skiing where there is plenty of room to turn where you want. But still, it's important. If you plant the pole too early in a turn, your body will start to turn before your feet do, and you'll wind up leaning in. Plant the pole too late and you'll find yourself back on your heels.

The pole plant is not a means of support, but rather a trigger to time the start of the turn. As we saw in the section on tactics, it is important in racing to make the turn in the right place if you want to line up correctly on the next gate.

In a race, if you plant the pole too early, you have to take action so that your feet don't turn. To keep the line you want, you try to let

the skis continue ahead on that line. But now your pole plant has started your body leaning downhill and you're off balance. On the other hand, if you do let the skis come around in the turn in a race, you wind up turning before the inside pole of the gate and may straddle it, hit it, or miss the gate entirely.

If you plant the pole too late, it's usually a simple case of being too late in making the turn. In order to be close to the inside pole of the gate, or wherever you want the turn to occur, the pole plant must be timed correctly.

Most recreational skiers make the mistake of swinging the pole and planting it ahead and too close to their skis. Try to plant the pole more downhill to improve your angulation in the completion phase and to pull yourself into the turn in the initiation phase. The steeper the hill, the more the pole should be planted laterally from the skier's body down the hill.

Sum-Up

Continue to practice the one-ski exercises shown in this book. Focus on independent leg action in your skiing. Pressure the outside ski in turning so that you carve, not skid, your turns. It is no longer acceptable, given the modern ski and boot, for people to slop their turns. Precise, carved turns are within the reach of everyone, and the model of the good ski racer is one the recreational skier can emulate with confidence.

NINE

THE BEST IN THE WORLD

For many years the Austrians dominated international ski racing. Then the French, led by Jean-Claude Killy, were on top. The Italians came next, and the Swiss—with their satellite ski team from Liechtenstein—have led the pack in recent years.

The U.S. Ski Team has yet to match the team strength of those countries, but it did have its glory years with the success of individual racers in 1982–84.

Phil won the World Cup in 1981, 1982, and 1983. In '82, he also won both the individual World Cup titles in slalom and giant slalom, while Steve won a gold medal at the World Championships. In 1982, too, the U.S. women's Alpine team was the best in the world, winning the female division of the Nations Cup. That was also the year when Bill Koch won the World Cup of cross-country skiing—a double triumph in Alpine and Nordic skiing.

The next winter Phil won his third World Cup while Tamara McKinney became the first U.S. woman to capture the World Cup. In 1984 the United States took three gold medals and two silver medals at the Sarajevo Olympics. Bill Johnson's win was sensational, not only because he became the first American man to win an Olympic gold medal in Alpine skiing, but also because he was the first to win any Olympic or World Championship race in downhill, and downhill previously had never been a strength of the U.S.

Ski Team. In fact, with Debby Armstrong's capture of the giant slalom gold medal at Sarajevo, and our win in the slalom, the U.S. Ski Team won medals in all three Alpine disciplines.

In contrast to 1981, when Phil struggled from the beginning and then to the last race in order to win the World Cup, he started the 1981–82 season in a stunning way:

"In December alone—before the Christmas break—I accumulated 135 points in seven races and two combined results. It was more than any racer had ever won in such a short time, and more than half of all the World Cup points I had earned in the entire previous season.

"Returning to Europe after Christmas, I continued to race well, placing second to Ingemar Stenmark three times and picking up another combined. On January 23, I won the slalom at Wengen over Stenmark. Statistically, he could no longer catch me. I had won the World Cup with 262 points and the season was only half over!"

From Wengen we traveled over to Schladming, the site of the 1982 World Alpine Ski Championships. It was not an easy time for

Steve. "Just before New Year's, my wife, Debbie, gave birth to our first child, Ginger, and I had to leave on January 3 to rejoin the World Cup tour. Riding up on the lift to the starts of races, I wondered what was going on at home. I'd wish I hadn't left them. I'd call home once or twice a week. Once Debbie told me that if I had called a week before I did at the World Championships, she would have asked me to come home.

"During the Christmas break, too, Dick Steadman had operated on my knees. Early in December, I had taken a bad fall in France and had developed a catching sensation in the right knee. Then the left knee started to swell and give me pain.

"Steadman performed arthroscopic surgery on both knees. From the left knee he removed cartilage. On the right leg he slipped the kneecap into a slightly different position by cutting a bit from the bands that line the joint.

Steve winning the giant slalom gold medal at the 1982 World Championships. "Those are gold medal knees," said Dick Steadman.

K2/TEAM RUSSELL

"I guess you could call the surgery minor, but Dick Steadman later said that he had awakened in the middle of the night and thought, 'I've just operated on that boy's knees with only six weeks to go before the World Championships!'

"What Steadman told me, though, was, 'Those are now gold medal knees.' He must have been gazing into a crystal ball.

"The hill for the giant slalom at Schladming was steep and rock hard. I started fourth, and had a super run. Stenmark seemed to experience some trouble with his edges, and came in a terrible 1.37 seconds behind me.

"Then Phil started. He had already won the World Cup and looked like he'd win this one. There was a huge crowd, but you could have heard the snow fall off a pine bough.

"I was waiting in the finish area, and within ten seconds I heard a terrible groan from the crowd. Phil had skied out of the course after only a few gates. Watching it on TV, it looked as though he crossed the tails of his skis after he got locked into a turn and couldn't transfer his weight to the new turning ski in time.

"In the second run Stenmark changed skis and was racing ahead of me. He had a super run. Even with the big lead I was carrying from the first run, I had cause for concern. Stenmark was the giant slalom gold medalist of Lake Placid and World Cup g.s. leader five out of six years. I had never even won a World Cup giant slalom race!

"Phil had studied Stenmark's run on TV in a room near the finish area. He radioed up to me that the course looked like it carried rounder turns than the first run, but I should ski aggressively.

"I did, and got into trouble on the fifth gate. It took me several gates to get back on course. I figured with the mistakes I was making, I'd be lucky to place third. But then I picked up the rhythm of the course and nailed the bottom half. I was .86 seconds slower than Stenmark, but it was good for gold. It also was the first World Championship race ever won by an American man.

"Before the race, Ed Chase, my ski service rep, had stuck a small strip of tape on my skis and written on it, 'Ginger 1.' I planned to win the race for my new daughter. At the finish I held up the skis and pointed at the tape. Everyone assumed I was trying to indicate that I'd won the gold medal on K2s.

"Actually, the skis I won on were not really mine."

In the summer of 1981, Phil had asked K2 to build a new variation of a giant slalom ski. We were constantly testing new skis, and K2 was constantly asking us, "What would happen if we tried this?"

At the time Phil was using a ski that had short pieces of aluminum in the bottom, fore and aft of the boot. The idea of the metal was to make the ski more stable at high speeds while making it lively. Phil asked the K2 people to run a whole other piece of metal along the top, along with the two bottom pieces fore and aft. The designers said it couldn't be done. The addition of the extra metal to the glass wrap, with the contraction and expansion rates of the other materials, would cause the ski to lose all its camber when it got cold.

"I don't care, I want you to do it!" Phil said to them.

"So they made up six pair. Of the six I liked only one pair really well, and I tossed them into the ski bag to take to Europe. But I didn't plan to use them because I didn't want to train on one construction and race on another."

That season Steve was skiing on a laminated ski that was more like a Rossignol or an Atomic, having a full metal top and bottom. "In the first race of the season, however, I crushed the sidewall on the ski. One pair was gone. Then I tried another pair and had trouble with those. Soon I had no skis of my own that I really liked.

"Suddenly the World Championships were coming up. I asked Ed Chase to give me more skis to try. Among them were the skis Phil had asked to be made up and which the designers said wouldn't work. We called them EL Combis. I chose them to race on.

"They were really a glass-wrapped construction, with an aluminum sheet laying over the top of the foam core, and then the fiberglass wrapped around all that. I skied on them for two days at Schladming. The third day I went out and won a gold medal on them! Then I used them to win two more giant slaloms that winter.

"I continued to race on the EL Combis, but eventually—as is the case with metal—I found they were too stiff torsionally."

When a ski is torsionally stiff it can cause the tip to hold too much in turning. Then the ski can't hold the pressure. This ski would jump off the edge instead of flattening out. It would bite and flip away.

We asked the designers to try cutting slits down the metal to soften the ski up torsionally. They did that, and we liked the new ski even better. But no one else seemed to be able to ski on it well, and it was never marketed as a recreational ski.

We used a model called the VO for five years before K2 felt they could bring it to market. The VO has a cracked steel edge designed to soften up the ski and make it hold on hard snow—not flutter or vibrate, but damp. It's really just a hard-snow ski, but skiers poured into ski shops to buy it because we raced on it.

As important to the success of a racer as equipment is the technical rep who prepares the skis for races. Almost from the beginning of our careers on the World Cup our tech rep was Ed Chase of K2. He came to us in 1976. After 1980 he used to say every spring, "This'll be my last year," but he stuck with us to the end in 1984. He said he'd stay on as long as we did, but we believe he would have retired after 1984 even if we had continued.

Our tech rep Ed Chase threatened to quit, but he always came back. Steve won a gold medal on skis Chase gave him only two days before the race.

Ed is a big guy with a handlebar mustache, a graduate of Middlebury College whose nickname is Sleez. Sleez's job was to file, stone, sandpaper, and wax our skis. He tuned our skis before a race and between runs. He also had to prepare the skis for transportation between events.

Before the race Sleez would carry our skis to the start while we were warming up on our training skis. About fifteen minutes before the start we would have him put the skis on and adjust the bindings. Then we made a few turns. If the edges felt too sharp, Sleez would dull them with emery paper. If they still felt too sharp—as they often did in giant slalom—he'd dull them a little more. Finally, he'd clean our goggles just before the start.

Wax selection for the race was totally Ed Chase's responsibility. He looked at the wax charts, inspected the snow on the race hill, figured the temperature changes between runs.

The tech reps on the World Cup are almost as competitive as the racers. Even within the U.S. Ski Team the Rossignol rep won't let the Atomic rep know what wax he's using for the race. The coaches may let the reps know how they think the racers' skis should be waxed, but the reps mostly do their own thing.

It may seem odd that the team isn't the ultimate authority on how skis for a major race are waxed, but the system really does work. First of all, the reps are more experienced than the racers or coaches in preparing skis. Secondly, waxing may be slightly different for one ski brand than another, depending on the construction of the ski. Thirdly, if the skis are waxed differently, there is less chance of the whole team being wrong in a single race. It's like hedging a bet.

Once, in a giant slalom in Japan, where the snow conditions are unlike any other place in the world, we were waxed so wrong that Phil had to get up out of a tuck on a flat section and pole his way to reach the next gate. Meanwhile, racers from other countries were rocketing across the flat. Schoenhaar, our coach, was fit to be tied. After that experience we often joked to Sleez, "We hope our skis are waxed better today than in Japan."

In fact, Sleez became one of the top tech reps in the world. Frequently, he helped other racers prepare their skis, even if they weren't K2s.

By the time the World Championships were over, four of the five medals won by the United States, including a combined bronze, went to a Mahre or to Christin Cooper, just as would happen at Sarajevo. In 1984, Christin retired along with us.

Phil had done nothing at the Schladming World Championships, falling in both races. But that experience served to fire him to a new determination: to win both the slalom and giant slalom World Cup titles. That was Stenmark territory, and it wouldn't be easy, but Phil was fixed on the idea that in 1982—no two ways about it—he was going to earn the title "best skier in the world."

"No one could say at that point that I had won the World Cup because of combined points that Stenmark lacked. Even if I had not won a single combined point earlier in the season, I would still have had an insurmountable lead for the overall World Cup.

"What I wanted more than anything was to take the slalom and g.s. titles away from Stenmark, who had held them for so many years. Without those titles people could say, 'Well, yes, Phil won the World Cup, but Ingemar still is the best technical skier in the world.'

"Never before, or after, in my life have I skied a longer or better string of slalom and g.s. races. And yet Ingemar was always there. Of eighteen technical races that winter, Ingemar and I finished first and second in half of them. I placed in the first three in seventeen out of the eighteen races.

"For some reason, just as he had lost the g.s. title to Steven at Schladming, Ingemar's giant slalom skiing began to falter toward the end of the season. Earlier he had the lead on me with three wins, while I had a string of six second-place finishes and wound up the season with 105 points out of a potential 125 in giant slalom. Ingemar never caught me, though. Either he DNF'd or didn't place in the top three in the final races coming down the stretch.

"The fight for the slalom title went all the way to the last race at a resort called Montgenèvre in the French Alps, where the finale of the World Cup took place. Prior to the race, I had recorded three firsts during the season in slalom, and two second places that counted. Ingemar had two firsts and three seconds to count. If he won at Montgenèvre, we would be tied for the slalom title. If I won, the title would be mine.

"The slalom hill at Montgenèvre was steep on top and it flattened toward the end. I liked that kind of transition. I also liked the way the flags had been set. I knew there was no one who could ski that race better than I.

"After so many years racing you get a feeling for the courses you can ski well on. If the flag settings were really tight, I'd throw up my hands and say, 'This is set for Stenmark. It's his kind of course.'

"I like courses that make the racer turn, with the gates not set too tightly together nor too far apart, and where there are changes in terrain and rhythm. You have to think on that kind of course.

"Montgenèvre was my kind of course.

"In the first run, though, a slalom pole had come out of the snow, and the gatekeeper had to stand there holding it up. It disturbed my rhythm. The officials offered me a rerun if I wanted to take one.

"Meanwhile, Stenmark had come in just 3/10ths of a second ahead of my time. It wasn't a big enough margin that I couldn't strike back. If I were to ski my first run again and hook a tip, I would be out of it. Better not gamble. So I declined the offer of the rerun and accepted my first-run result.

"I was really up for the second run. My confidence had never been higher. I knew from the end of the steep to the finish that I would take a second and a half away from anyone in the world. And I won the race and the World Cup slalom title.

"The next day, on the same hill, they held the parallel slalom race, the one always staged at the end of the World Cup season. Ingemar and I wound up as finalists, and again I beat him. There wasn't anyone in the world who was going to beat me at ski racing in those very special days.

"After the parallel they presented the World Cup trophies, and three times I climbed onto the outdoor stage—to collect the giant

When Phil won the World Cup in 1981, and Steve was fourth, all of Yakima turned out for the homecoming parade.

FRANK B. DENMAN

slalom trophy, the slalom, and then my second overall World Cup.

"It was great, too, to see the whole U.S. women's team up there receiving *SKI* magazine's Nations Cup award for leading all the other countries in the world in women's ski racing.

"On top of that, over in Italy, Bill Koch, like me, had to go all the way down to the last race of the season to win the cross-country World Cup. It was some kind of day for the U.S. Ski Team.

"In addition, I had won the combined title in the World Cup.

"That summer I worked hard to finish the house I had begun outside of Yakima. I had bought a nice hillside overlooking the Yakima River, which flows into the Columbia, about eighty miles downstream. A rough road led up the hill to the building site.

"Previous years in Europe there were many hours between races when I had nothing to do. I doodled on paper or designed in my mind a house I would build someday. It was like a dream going through my head. I knew exactly where I wanted the bedrooms, how the living area would look with its high, vaulted ceiling.

"With the help of other friends, we built most of the house ourselves. The only work I subcontracted was the masonry, heating system, and Sheetrock. We kept changing the house as we went along, moving a wall here, altering a room there.

"Building the house was absorbing and left me little time to think about anything else, even the sports we enjoyed and which helped our conditioning. At home I normally play basketball several times a week. We dirt-bike and go water skiing. Andy Mill, one of the downhillers on the ski team, came once to stay with us in Yakima. When he went home he told everyone that 'If you played as hard as the Mahres do you'd be in shape too.' Steve and I were never big on pure physical conditioning. One time the ski team gave us a conditioning program to follow. Push-ups and so on. We were required to run the 440 in a certain time. I did it twice. In the middle of the third 440, I gave up. That year I won the first World Cup race of the season in France.

Our love of speed carried over into dirt-bike racing during the summer; here, Steve's in front.   TOM LIPPERT

"People say we won because we were gifted skiers. Maybe, yet we also found that the best training for skiing is skiing itself. Nothing else uses the same muscles. But if you can't ski, you should stay active in other sports.

"Our lack of activity working on the house in the summer of '82 may have affected my skiing that fall. Then, when I arrived at Copper Mountain for November training, matters weren't helped when I went into the first team meeting. As usual it was to discuss rules, regulations, dress code. I was singled out for wearing a Levi's shirt that wasn't from one of the team sponsors while being interviewed for T.V. Suddenly it brought back all the bad things about life on the team. They were trying to dominate my life, and I resented it.

"It also was the first season of the Super G. Everywhere I went I was pursued by people wanting to know why I refused to race in it,

For Phil, building a new house became an obsession. "Lack of training wrecked the beginning of my 1982–83 season."

TOM LIPPERT

how I expected to win the World Cup again without competing in it. With two of the Super G's linked to downhill races for combineds, I had the potential to sacrifice at least fifty World Cup points by not competing. I would just as soon have lost the World Cup, though, than give up what I believed in. And I did not believe the Super G was good for ski racing.

"The Alps had a snow problem at the beginning of the 1982–83 season, and races were switched from one place to another. The travel and waiting around were tedious. By Christmas break I had only thirty points and ranked seventeenth in the World Cup standings.

"When I returned to Europe in January, neither the weather nor my skiing improved much. At Adelboden, Switzerland, in the first giant slalom of the season, a young comer named Pirmin Zurbriggen won and took the lead in the World Cup."

Zurbriggen is the best all-round skier to appear for years on the World Cup. In 1984–85 he won a slalom, g.s., *and* a downhill race, which hasn't been done by a man on the World Cup in years.

If anything, Zurbriggen is even more shy than Stenmark. After he won the Adelboden race, he was asked what he thought his chances of winning the World Cup were.

"I can see it in one eye," he replied. From that point on, the season went downhill for Zurbriggen, and the racers took to calling him "the one-eyed bandit." We used to say that he was no longer racing well because he was skiing with only one eye; the other was on the World Cup. But he got his revenge on us all the next season when he won the World Cup in 1984.

In mid-January, Phil's wife, Holly, and daughter, Lindsey, joined him on the tour. "People were critical, thinking that the presence of my family would distract me. I sure proved them wrong. At the Hahnenkamm, I placed twelfth and thirteenth in two downhills, I was third in the slalom, picked up twenty-five points for first place in the combined, and suddenly I was standing eighth in the World Cup. Two weeks later I had the best downhill result of my life in the Arlberg Kandahar at St. Anton. Together with my third in the A-K slalom, I picked up another twenty-five combined points.

Switzerland's Pirmin
Zurbriggen would win the
World Cup after Phil.
We called him "the
one-eyed bandit," but
he fooled us all.

ASPEN SKIING CO.

"In two days at St. Anton, I picked up fifty-one World Cup points and was standing first in the World Cup!

"A few days later we moved to Garmisch in Germany, and I stayed out of another Super G. I thought Stenmark was with me in boycotting the Super G, but evidently he was desperate for points, so he entered. To me it was just like his entry in the downhill at Kitzbühel, his one and only. He had said all along he would never run downhill, and there he was competing. I thought he made a fool of himself, even though it gave him combined points.

Now here he was in the Super G, which he also said he wouldn't enter. Personally, I think he was under pressure from his factories to compete and produce. It didn't do him much good. He placed only eleventh.

"Meanwhile, my skiing was picking up. I was starting to feel my timing and the line. I felt more comfortable on my skis.

"We returned to the States in early March. At Aspen, I placed ninth in the downhill. The next day I won the giant slalom. Mathematically, I had won my third World Cup!

"At Vail, I went on to beat Stenmark in a giant slalom. We then flew to Japan, where I won another g.s. So I retained my World Cup giant slalom title as well. And I led the combined.

"A special thrill at the final World Cup ceremonies at Furano, Japan, was to receive the World Cup with Tamara McKinney of the U.S. Not only did she become the first American woman to win the World Cup, but our double win impressed the world that America was on top in ski racing."

Tamara comes from a strong skiing family too. Her sister, Sheila, raced on the ski team, and her brother, Steve, held the world speed record. He was the first man to go over 200 kilometers an hour on skis.

When Steve Mahre first met Tamara she was the tiniest ski racer he'd ever seen. " 'How can an eighty-pound kid compete against bigger women, four or five years older?' I asked myself. I thought it would destroy her. But she had the determination to succeed.

"Tamara tried more than the other women to imitate things the guys were doing. Tom Kelly, a coach on the U.S. Ski Team, once heard her say that what she'd really like to do was to 'train with Phil and Steve so I can run slalom the way they do.' She never did, but she had plenty of time to watch us ski.

"Tamara would seek out new things to help her skiing. She was prepared to try new things, and that's not true of a lot of women who are content with the way they ski. Unless a coach, or someone, suggests they try a different tack, most women won't initiate a change themselves. Tamara tried more than the others to imitate the guys, attempting to capture the quickness and aggressiveness of their skiing."

In size and temperament, Tamara was the opposite of Annemarie Moser-Proell, the greatest woman ski racer in history. Proell was a big lady, with more desire and aggression than any woman on the tour. She even looked tough.

Greatest woman ski racer
of all time, Annemarie Proell,
is seen with her World
Cups. *KRISTIAN BISSUTI*

We can remember Proell and her sidekick on the Austrian Team, Monika Kaserer, smoking cigarettes in the finish area. Annemarie didn't look like an athlete to us. But she had what it takes. She retired, then came back and was as good as ever.

McKinney, Proell, Mittermaier . . . Stenmark, Zurbriggen . . . they're all different. They pose the question to which there seems to be no definitive answer: What does it take to be the best skier in the world?

Ski racing is a difficult sport. It is tougher than tennis, for example, in the sense that an Ingemar Stenmark must be able to master more skills than a Bjorn Borg. Borg plays on a tennis court where the dimensions of the playing area are always the same, the net the same height. For Stenmark every race is different. The flags are set differently, the terrain is different, the snow conditions vary.

And the top skiers have to master different disciplines—and they have to adjust constantly.

Many kids in ski racing today would ski better if they not only skied more events but played other sports. The true athlete is someone who, if he puts his mind to it, can excel in any sport he wants. It was always important to us to do well in sports other than just skiing.

The management of the ski associations and many coaches are forever trying to concoct foolproof programs to bring kids up to be champions. But you just can't take a kid who has talent and write an insurance policy that says he is going to be a champion. He won't be a winner if he doesn't want it. Without ambition he'll lack the mental attitude and the drive to go places.

Some kids blame their failures on coaching or structured ski programs. On the other hand, it wasn't ski team coaches who made Phil into a three-event skier and who could will him to win the World Cup.

"I *wanted* to win the World Cup. I was ready to take any chance to do that."

If a country wants to win the World Cup, it is first going to have to have a racer who wants to win the World Cup.

A country can't determine to win the Nations Cup, either. Individual racers don't think about winning the Nations Cup for their national ski team. What each racer has to do is to think about what he or she can do to win a race themselves. The Nations Cup is something that happens if a ski team has a lot of racers, in depth, who think that way. A couple of guys like the Mahres couldn't win the Nations Cup for America. There had to be more of us.

It gets back to having enough racers with the mental strength to make sacrifices to win. The Canadians did it with their downhill team. At first they were just a bunch of ordinary skiers who thought they had a better chance to do well in downhill than in the technical races. They trained, they had guts and desire, and they went out and did it.

Training for downhill alone, though, isn't the solution to being a true champion in skiing. Nor is thinking about winning a gold medal at the Olympics. The slalom we won at Sarajevo was the only ski race we won that entire winter. It had to be due to some luck, or a little help from upstairs, but it wasn't something you could program for.

"Bring home the gold, bring home the gold!" you hear people shout. But they don't have any idea what they're asking. Athletic programs that put stress on young people to try for that kind of winning simply are misdirected.

The trend to specialization in ski racing, we believe, is really wrong. The goal should be to succeed in the World Cup as an all-round skier. To do this a kid should learn to ski fast, unhampered by a lot of technique. The goal then should be to become a two-event skier, in slalom and giant slalom. It's impossible to be a downhiller and branch off from there.

You do have to pick kids, though, capable of skiing with no fear at all. Everyone has fear, but they have to be able to ski so fast that they will one day enter a World Cup downhill and find it a breeze.

Skiing fast and having a powerful will to succeed—if it were possible to create such things, someone would have figured a way by now. We believe that they're attributes born in skiers—even, sometimes, two at a time.

We're family people, and bringing wives and children to races picked us up. Will
our kids race and win?

LORI ADAMSKI-PEEK